A Fugitive from Utopia

A Fugitive from Utopia

THE POETRY OF ZBIGNIEW HERBERT

STANISLAW BARANCZAK

HARVARD UNIVERSITY PRESS
Cambridge, Massachusetts, and London, England   1987

This book is printed on acid-free paper, and its binding
materials have been chosen for strength and durability.

Library of Congress Cataloging-in-Publication Data

Barańczak, Stanisław, 1946–
    A fugitive from Utopia.

    Translation of: Uciekinier z Utopii.
    Includes index.
    1. Herbert, Zbigniew—Criticism and interpretation.
I. Title.
PG7167.E64Z5913   1987   891.8′517   86-25818
ISBN 0-674-32685-7

Designed by Gwen Frankfeldt

To Adam Michnik

Acknowledgments

SEVERAL parts of this book have appeared, under different titles and in abbreviated form, in periodicals: "Zbigniew Herbert's 'Unmasking Metaphor,'" *Cross Currents* 4 (1985); "Zbigniew Herbert and the Concept of Poetic Irony," *Russian Literature* 16 (1984); "The Limits of Irony: Zbigniew Herbert's Imponderabilia," *Manhattan Review* 2 (Winter 1984/85). The book itself is a slightly abbreviated version of my *Uciekinier z Utopii: O poezji Zbigniewa Herberta* (London: Polonia Book Fund, 1984).

My thanks are due to Richard Lourie and Camille Smith for their editorial help, Aleksander Fiut for his reading of the manuscript and valuable comments, and Clare Cavanagh for her devoted assistance throughout my research.

I am grateful for permission to quote Herbert's poetry and prose from the following works:

Selected Poems, translated by John and Bogdana Carpenter (1977), copyright © 1977 by John and Bogdana Carpenter, reprinted by permission of Oxford University Press.

Report from the Besieged City, translated by John and Bogdana Carpenter, copyright © 1985 by Zbigniew Herbert. Published by The Ecco Press in 1985. Reprinted by permission of The Ecco Press.

Selected Poems, translated by Czeslaw Milosz and Peter Dale Scott, copyright © 1968 by Zbigniew Herbert, translation copyright © 1968 by Czeslaw Milosz and Peter Dale Scott. Reprinted by permission of Penguin Books Ltd. and The Ecco Press.

"Report from the Besieged City," reprinted by permission from *The New York Review of Books,* copyright © 1983 Nyrev, Inc.

"Pebble" and "From Mythology," published in *The Observer,* 2 September 1962. Reprinted by permission of *The Observer.*

Postwar Polish Poetry, selected and translated by Czeslaw Milosz, copyright © 1965 by Czeslaw Milosz. Reprinted by permission of Doubleday and Company, Inc.

Contents

A Fugitive from Utopia

Throughout the book I quote Zbigniew Herbert's poems only in English translation. Each quotation is followed by a double reference to both the Polish and the English or American editions in which the poem appeared for the first time. In these references I use the following abbreviations:

SS   *Struna światła* (Warsaw, 1956)
H   *Hermes, pies i gwiazda* (Warsaw, 1957)
SP   *Studium przedmiotu* (Warsaw, 1961)
N   *Napis* (Warsaw, 1969)
P   *Pan Cogito* (Warsaw, 1974)
R   *Raport z oblężonego miasta i inne wiersze* (Paris, 1983)
M   *Selected Poems,* trans. Czeslaw Milosz and Peter Dale Scott (Harmondsworth: Penguin, 1968)
C   *Selected Poems,* trans. John Carpenter and Bogdana Carpenter (Oxford: Oxford University Press, 1977)
CR   *Report from the Besieged City and Other Poems,* trans. John Carpenter and Bogdana Carpenter (New York: Ecco Press, 1985).

Where neither M, C, nor CR is mentioned, the English translation is by Richard Lourie, whose collaboration is warmly appreciated.

Introduction

THERE is no doubt that, at this writing, Zbigniew Herbert is the most admired and respected poet now living in Poland. His fame has been growing steadily since his debut in 1956 and reached a peak in the years following the imposition of martial law in 1981. Polish readers have always revered poets who succeed in defining the nation's spiritual dilemmas; what is exceptional in Herbert is that his popularity at home is matched by a wide acclaim abroad. His work, which has occasioned numerous brilliant comments from both Polish and Western critics,[1] yields relatively well to translation and is available almost in its entirety in most Western languages, including English.[2] It seems as if this particular poet has managed to find a magical formula for an equilibrium between what is nationally or historically specific and what is universal and timeless.

One is tempted to say that Herbert found the formula himself as much as it found him. What is this formula? What makes Herbert's poetic voice unique and meaningful is a fundamental contradiction between his attachment to the values of Western cultural "heritage" and his awareness of the Eastern European's irreversible state of "disinheritance." The popular image of Herbert, especially in Polish criticism of the late 1950s and the 1960s, has more often than not been that of a modern Classicist—a poet of the West, the past, and culture.[3] Yet a careful reading of his work makes one realize that this apparent Classicist is, at the same time, an Eastern European "barbarian"—a poet of Poland, our age, and tangible experience. This uneasy balance or, rather, this persistent sense of incurable duality is by no means an abstract notion; on the contrary, it has its roots in the poet's personal encounters with twentieth-century history in the making. Therefore, a knowledge of Herbert's biography is crucial to an understanding of his work.[4]

Zbigniew Herbert was born on November 29, 1924, in Lvov; his father was a lawyer, a bank director, and a professor of economics. The date and place of birth and the family background are all significant. Herbert's complicated genealogy—his ancestors included an English great-grandfather and an Armenian grandmother, but the family had been culturally Polish for generations—symbolized, in a way, the ethnic, cultural, and religious syncretism of the city where he spent his early youth. Those were, however, the last years of Lvov as a Polish city. As a fifteen-year-old, Herbert experienced the annexation of his home town by the Soviet Union, one of the two powers which, on the strength of the Molotov-Ribbentropp Pact, had partitioned Independent Poland. That experience proved crucial in both Herbert's life and his poetry. As a high school student in Lvov, he attempted to found an illegal organization called "White Eagle," which was "promptly caught"—his first encounter with the police machine of a totalitarian state.[5] As a poet in postwar Poland, he eventually wrote a few poems—"The Country" (H 115), "September 17" (R 69, CR 63), and others—that cannot be understood without reference to the events of 1939.[6]

After the German invasion in 1941 Lvov found itself under Nazi occupation. Herbert (whose father's brother had been executed by the Soviets in Katyn forest)[7] graduated from a clandestine high school study group. In the last years of the war he took part in the Home Army's underground activities, while studying Polish language and literature at a clandestine university. After 1944, when Lvov was once again captured by the Soviets, he lived in Cracow, where he studied painting for a while but eventually graduated in 1947 from the local Academy of Commerce with a master's degree in economics. A vacillation between "practical," down-to-earth majors and artistic or philosophical interests was characteristic of his moves during the next years, when he studied law and philosophy, among other subjects, in Torun and Warsaw—philosophy under the supervision of an outstanding non-Marxist thinker, Henryk Elzenberg, to whom he would later dedicate one of his best-known poems, "To Marcus Aurelius."[8]

It was during the first few years after the war that Herbert had—despite his politically damaging Home Army past—some opportunity to become involved in Poland's new literary life (or, more precisely, to join its Catholic current, which, in any case, was gradually being pushed off to the side). In fact, during that time he managed to make his debut as a poet and critic in the literary press and to establish close contact with the circle around *Tygodnik Powszechny* [The Universal Weekly].⁹ For Polish literature, the years 1944–1948 were still a phase of relative and limited pluralism, one proof of which was precisely the existence of *Tygodnik Powszechny,* a high-level Catholic cultural magazine with a pronounced antitotalitarian political orientation. The year 1949, however, marked the beginning of a new phase, in which Socialist Realism was officially forced upon writers and there was increasing harassment of independent publishing. *Tygodnik Powszechny* somehow survived, but not for very long. In 1953, after its editors refused, unlike those of all the other Polish magazines, to publish an idolatrous obituary of Joseph Stalin,¹⁰ the Communist authorities simply took the weekly from the independent Catholics and gave it to the proregime Catholic group PAX.

The years of Socialist Realism triumphant were a period in which Herbert was almost totally absent from literary life—or rather, refused to participate in it. In 1951 he even resigned from the official Polish Writers' Union. (The only other prominent poet to act similarly was another excellent author of the same generation, Miron Białoszewski.) Herbert—who escaped the threat of being conscripted as a military prosecutor—took various odd jobs, accessible to him because of his degree in economics, to earn his living in the early 1950s. He was respectively an editor on the Gdansk economic journal *Przegląd Kupiecki* [Merchant Review], a bank clerk, a shop attendant, an accountant and timekeeper in a cooperative, a designer of sanitation gear and protective wear in a certain Bureau of Research and Projects for the Peat Industry, and, finally—after the political "thaw" of the mid-1950s—an administrator in the Association of Polish Composers. During the years of Stalinism, Herbert's jobs were extremely underpaid and the poet lived on the margin. Despite his extreme poverty, however, he stubbornly refused to join the Socialist Realist mainstream that was the official culture in those times. Thirty years later he confessed: "I didn't have even a glimmer of hope of surviving, even physically, because that was quite a hard time for me . . . I was absolutely certain that I would perish but I wouldn't take the easy way, wouldn't accept any kind of collaboration. I resigned from the Writer's Union at that time, no one threw me out."¹¹ A recently published diary written in 1954 by Herbert's friend the novelist Leopold Tyrmand, who was himself then in a similar situation, provides some additional details of interest:

> Herbert visited me this afternoon. He's one of the best of my contemporaries . . . Of course, he's down and out. He earns several hundred zlotys a month as an accountant-timekeeper in a cooperative that produces paper bags, toys, or boxes. The serenity with which Herbert endures that drudgery—him, a man with degrees in three fields—is straight from Early Christian hagiography. That serenity is a carefully crafted mask—it conceals the despair of a man who fears that he gambled away his life in History's absurd game of poker, where the stakes were honor and ideological attachments.

> Zbyszek [Herbert] came here this morning for a chat. He's changing jobs . . ."I've had enough, I can't go on like this. Do you know what it means to be in charge of recording the productivity of the pitiful remains of what was once a human being, who smiles at me toothlessly, because a few figures written down by me can decide whether he gets another bowl of soup in his life . . . And he looks at me with watery eyes that once read Schopenhauer . . . That's it. I quit . . ." I knew the difficulties he had to overcome to get that job and so I said with no enthusiasm: "What are you going to do, then?" "I have a prospect," said Herbert, "in the Central Peat Industry Bureau. That's the place for me." Pensioners, invalids, peatbogs—Herbert's metaphysics of personality. His intensive training in despair.

> Herbert read his new poems this evening. Looks as though working in peat is having a fertilizing influence on him. There is nothing to do there, you can't read newspapers during the office hours, so Zbyszek sits at his desk and writes poems and fables. Everybody thinks he's an exemplary and zealous worker, while Zbyszek struggles with his obsession—that of a wasted life, which, as we know, is the best fertilizer for poetry.[12]

Years later Herbert would, significantly, explain his refusal to participate by citing aesthetic and not moral considerations. One of his most recent poems, "The Power of Taste," reads as follows:

> It didn't require great character at all
> our refusal disagreement and resistance
> we had a shred of necessary courage
> but fundamentally it was a matter of taste
>   Yes taste
> in which there are fibers of soul the cartilage of
>   conscience
>
> Who knows if we had been better and more
>   attractively tempted
> sent rose-skinned women thin as a wafer
> or fantastic creatures from the paintings of
>   Hieronymus Bosch
> but what kind of hell was there at this time
> a wet pit the murderers' alley the barrack
> called a palace of justice
> a home-brewed Mephisto in a Lenin jacket
> sent Aurora's grandchildren out into the field
> boys with potato faces
> very ugly girls with red hands
>
> . . . . .
>
> So aesthetics can be helpful in life
> one should not neglect the study of beauty
>
> Before we declare our consent we must carefully
>   examine
> the shape of the architecture the rhythm of the drums
>   and pipes
> official colors the despicable ritual of funerals
>
> > Our eyes and ears refused obedience
> > the princes of our senses proudly chose exile
> > (R 75–76, CR 69)

Although Stalin's death might have been the immediate cause of the loss of *Tygodnik Powszechny,* viewed in general, the situation of Polish culture after 1953 underwent gradual relaxation. The new developments that timidly presaged the approaching "thaw" made it possible for Herbert to resurface in the literary press. The anthology *Każdej chwili wybierać muszę* [I Have to Choose at Any Moment], published under Catholic auspices in 1954, contains a handful of his poems. The year 1955 marked his second debut in literary magazines. The collective presentation of five poets (Miron Białoszewski, Stanisław Czycz, Bohdan Drozdowski, Jerzy Harasymowicz, Zbigniew Herbert) in one of the December 1955 issues of the weekly *Życie Literackie* [Literary Life] was much discussed and of great consequence for the further development of Polish poetry. The next year, a year particularly rich both in political and literary events, saw Herbert's first book, the volume *Struna światła* [Chord of Light]. It was acclaimed by the critics and the literary public as one of the more sensational debuts of the "wave" of 1956, which also included first books by Białoszewski, Harasymowicz, and Stanisław Grochowiak. This period, along with the external circumstances and the inward perplexity that accompanied Herbert's debut, was soon reflected in such poems as the famous "Drawer" (SP 32–33, M 89, C 32).

Herbert's fame grew rapidly during the next years, especially after the publication of the volume *Hermes, pies i gwiazda* [Hermes, Dog and Star] in 1957 and the collection *Studium przedmiotu* [Study of the Object] in 1961. In 1958 the poet began a series of foreign travels through Western Europe, mostly France and Italy, recapitulated in his famous collection of essays of 1962, *Barbarzyńca w ogrodzie* [Barbarian in the Garden]. In 1961 Herbert was symbolically elected the Prince of Poets at the Student Culture Festival in Gdansk.

Since the early 1960s Herbert has met with increasingly profuse translation and comment abroad. After being awarded the prestigious Lenau Prize, he spent the years 1965–1971 in the West[13]—in Austria, France, West Germany, Greece, and the United States.[14] He left Poland again in 1973 in connection with receiving the Austrian Herder Prize and stayed away for a longer spell, residing mostly in West Berlin. This was a time of mounting hostility toward Herbert from the official managers of Poland's cultural policy, especially after December 1975 when his signature appeared on a letter of protest by Polish intellectuals against the constitutional amendments planned by the Communist Party.[15] Immediately upon his most recent return to Poland in early 1981, Herbert joined the editorial board of the uncensored literary quarterly *Zapis* [The Record]; another underground quarterly, *Krytyka* [Criticism], published an extensive interview with him (done by Adam Michnik in September 1980), in which the poet expressed, among other things, his hopes for the Poland of Solidarity. Herbert was in Poland—where he still resides at this writing—when martial law was imposed on December 13, 1981. His most recent book, *Raport z oblężonego miasta* [Report from the Besieged City], which includes, in addition to earlier work, several poems that deal with Poland's present situation, was the first of his books to be initially published abroad, by an émigré publishing house.

ONE

Antinomies

THE POETRY of Zbigniew Herbert is based on permanent confrontation—the confrontation of the Western tradition with the experience of an inhabitant of Eastern Europe, of the past with the present age, of cultural myth with the material particulars of life. But Herbert's "implied author"[1] is most often classified in popular opinion as a "Westernophile," someone who praises the past, and a poet of culture. By referring, in the Introduction, to the poet's biography, I have tried to suggest that the matter in question is by no means either obvious or simple. A scrupulous reading of the poems, focusing on an analysis of the antinomies that underpin Herbert's imagery, will, I hope, support my thesis that Herbert could just as easily be called a "barbarian," a poet of modern times and eulogist of the empirical concrete, as a poet of the Mediterranean, the past, and culture. Critics or readers who are immune to this fundamental duality of the poet resemble (no offense intended) the policemen from Herbert's poem "Georg Heym—the Almost Metaphysical Adventure," who are faced with a fact that transcends their way of thinking:

> licking their pencils
> they tried to record the event
> to introduce order
> according to the obsolete
> logic of Aristotle   (P 63, C 56)

Although the sense of this sentence in the poem is ironic—Herbert in fact wistfully defends this kind of logic, and his lyrical persona has always "adored tautologies [and] explanations *idem per idem*" (R 22, CR 17)—it is also true that Aristotelian logic often fails when applied to poetry. Its basic tenet, that a thing cannot be both "A" and "not-A," is particularly useless here. Herbert's poetry is a case in point: its implied author appears precisely as both "A" (a man attached to Western values, turned toward the past, and glorifying culture) and "not-A" (a man stigmatized by his Eastern provenance, focused on his own time, and assuming an extremely empirical point of view). He brings to mind the god Janus who looked simultaneously in two opposite directions. During a certain literary debate, Herbert remarked casually, "A poet's sphere of activity is not the time in which he lives but reality, which is a much broader notion."[2] The subject of his own work is reality in this specific sense, the reality that spreads between opposed extremes of values.

The ambivalent tension between opposed poles, a continuous "dialectic interplay of attitudes,"[3] has been Herbert's hallmark since his earliest poems. Let us begin with one highly characteristic example. The first volume by Herbert included the poem "Wawel" (SS 67), dedicated—in a meaningful gesture that complemented its underlying message—to Jerzy Turowicz, the editor-in-chief of *Tygodnik Powszechny*. This particular poem is rarely translated, and no wonder—it would be incomprehensible to a non-Pole unless provided with footnotes that would make clear its historical and cultural allusions. Not all these allusions are immediately comprehensible to the average Polish reader, either. Everybody in Poland knows that Wawel is the former royal castle in Cracow; a minimum knowledge of history lets the reader recall, in addition, that Wawel's past included moments of glory (in particular, its role as a symbol of the Golden Age of Renaissance culture in the second half of the sixteenth century) as well as degradation (for instance, the fact that during the era of partitions the Austrian authorities converted the castle into military barracks). Not everyone, however, will remember that Stanisław Wyspiański, the most prominent playwright of the fin-de-siècle movement Young Poland, based his drama *Akropolis* on a symbolic parallel between Wawel and the ancient Acropolis. Even fewer readers will know that after the Austrian military command had returned the castle in 1904 to institutions of Polish self-government in Galicia, Wyspiański had quite specific plans to rebuild Wawel into a modern Polish Acropolis in Pericleian style as a seat for parliamentary agencies and artistic or scientific institutions. Wyspiański (who was an artist as well as a writer) even started sketching some architectonic designs.[4] It is Wyspiański and his vision that are referred to by the principal allusion of the poem, introduced in its very first lines:

> He who made you equal to the marble edifice
> had a patriotic cataract in his eyes
>
> O Pericles
> how sad must your column feel
> and the straight shadow the dignity of capitals
> the harmony of raised arms
>
> While here—bricks in comic turmoil
> the royal orb of Renaissance
> against a background of Austrian barracks
>
> And perhaps only at night in a fever
> in madness in grief for a barbarian
> who has learned architectural symmetry
> from crosses and gallows
>
> and perhaps only under the moon
> when angels move away from the altar
> in order to trample dreams
>
> and only then
> it is an Acropolis
>
>> An Acropolis for the disinherited
>> and mercy mercy for liars

We must be aware of the nature of the polemics in this poem, polemics whose philosophical connotations far transcend the specific allusion to Wyspiański. Herbert cannot accept Wyspiański's "equalization" of the two uncontiguous worlds. What he enhances instead is the dissonance—the dissonance between the world symbolized by Pericles' name and the world of an Eastern European (Polish) "barbarian," between the world of universal Mediterranean myth and that of a particular national history, between harmony and suffering, between the lucid and dignified simplicity and the incoherent "comic turmoil." This confrontation, incidentally, is characteristically reflected in the syntax of the original: the harmonious and slightly archaic construction of sentences in the first six lines is contrasted with the more colloquial and disorderly syntax of the rest of the poem.

In any case, the poem's point is that "equalization" of the two opposed worlds is possible only within the realm of self-delusion; it can be carried out only by someone who is unable to perceive reality soberly and precisely because he has "a patriotic cataract in his eyes" and sees the world "in a fever," "in madness," "in grief," through the veil of "night" and "dream." In fact, the only sphere of harmony and equilibrium in the life of a Polish "barbarian" is, ironically, the gloomy geometry of "crosses and gallows" that surrounds him; therefore, only a "liar" who deliberately deludes himself can perceive an Acropolis in the Wawel castle. What's significant, though, is that in the last line this kind of delusion is not entirely mocked or condemned, since it is the only form of "mercy" within the reach of "liars."[5] Even more meaningful is Herbert's use of the word "disinherited" (*wydziedziczeni*), which deserves being pinpointed as the central notion within the poem. A "disinherited" individual, a northern "barbarian" of modern times, cut off from the sources of Pericleian harmony, has been separated from them against his will, forcibly—after all, nobody disinherits himself. And, like everyone who has been deprived of his inheritance against his will, he claims—albeit helplessly and ineffectively—his right to his "heritage."[6]

The theme of disinheritance,[7] bereavement,[8] expatriation, banishment from a symbolic Arcadia or Paradise Lost is indeed the central topic of Herbert's work. This theme was raised in early Herbert criticism,[9] but it is still underestimated in wider opinion. It is no accident that the constantly recurring self-definition of the implied author of these poems is "an exiled Arcadian" (H 47) or "an exile of obvious forms" (SS 40); it is no accident, either, that a mention of the literal "lifelong exile" of Thucydides is accompanied by a restrained but much more universal reflection: "exiles of all times / know what price that is" (N 51, M 137). In the case of "Wawel," this basic motif assumes several shapes at once: it is shown as the opposition between the West and Poland, between antiquity and modern history, between the harmony of myth and the suffering brought by reality. In many other poems by Herbert, the fundamental confrontation between the area of heritage and the area of disinheritance is carried out in a similarly multifaceted or multilayered manner. For analytic reasons, however, we may distinguish certain specific oppositions within the framework of this central motif. As I have already mentioned, three oppositions of this kind seem to play a leading role in Herbert's poetry. These are, to put it briefly, the oppositions of the *place, time,* and *source* of an experience. In other words, the confrontation is very often arranged along the lines of "the West versus the East," "the past versus the present," and "myth versus empiricism."

The West versus the East

I use the notions of "West" and "East" here, obviously, as conventional abbreviations without regard for geographic precision. There are poems, like "Wawel," in which the opposition of "South" versus "North" would be more appropriate; there are also others in which the notions of "Europe" versus "Poland" would be more accurate.[10] The opposed terms are, in addition, heavy with various meanings, not only geographic ones: they symbolize the opposition of cultural traditions, courses of history, political systems, even atmospheres of everyday life (contrasting the mythical luxury and exoticism of Europe or the wide world in general with the grayness of Polish everyday existence). The geographic opposition often coincides with the contrast between motion and immobility, traveling and staying put. In one of the latest poems, "Prayer of Mr. Cogito—Traveller" (R 17–18, CR 12–13), the chance to travel is thus symbolically identified with the chance to "understand" the world and with "humility" in the face of its diversity. Let us turn, however, to earlier examples. The prose poem "Fotoplastikon" (H 175), for instance, seems to be a particularly interesting statement from the point of view of the geographic confrontation:

> A huge brown barrel, into which they pour from
> above the Parisian blue, the Arabic silver, and the En-
> glish green. They add a pinch of the Indian pink as
> well and stir everything with a big scoop. Thick liquid
> oozes out through cracks, and the people who sit like
> flies round the barrel greedily lick up every drop. Un-
> fortunately, however, it doesn't last long. A streetcar,
> an ironic transatlantic liner, rings for the dreamers.

This prose poem has already been interpreted, very one-sidedly indeed, by the critic Artur Sandauer, who has trivialized its meaning by reducing it to the author's dreams of traveling abroad during the years when such travels were beyond his reach. "It is a crowd of local inhabitants," explains Sandauer, "who, while waiting at a streetcar stop, fix their eyes greedily on some Travel Agency which advertises unattainable trips abroad. Who knows, maybe we'll notice there (after all, these are only the 1950s) the poet himself?"[11] If this simplistic explanation reveals anything, it is that the critic does not understand "Fotoplastikon" on the most basic level, namely what is actually described and what it looks like. There is no trace in the poem of any streetcar stop or travel agency; Herbert's metaphoric description depicts quite faithfully a specific entertainment enterprise called in Polish *fotoplastikon,* which could be translated as "peep show" (although with no pornographic implication). It is a miniature theater for watching slides, technologically obsolete but still to be found in many Polish cities. Its cylindrical casing indeed resembles a barrel; the "cracks" are built-in peepholes, through which several people at once can watch slides, usually scenic views from exotic countries. This metaphor invites further associations. If the "thick liquid" of tempting views "oozes out through cracks," it can only mean that to admire them is to break a taboo, to commit a usurpation; in fact, they do not belong to "people," just as the honey in someone's breakfast does not belong to flies. An Eastern European "barbarian," to use the title metaphor from Herbert's collection of essays once again, can only steal into the "garden" of the exotic wide world and will never become a full-fledged citizen of it. In this light, Sandauer's one-dimensional interpretation of "Fotoplastikon" as the author's complaints about his passport or monetary problems appears senseless. What is at issue here is not only the technical impossibility of traveling, not only the clash between the fleeting dream and all too concrete reality; we can also assume that even with passports and money in their pockets the anonymous characters in the poem would still be pursued by their own mentality, which has been shaped by the experiences previously accessible to them.[12] Between exotic myth and homely reality there is the same kind of distance as between a transatlantic liner and a streetcar—the latter "ringing for the dreamers" and thus reminding them, even in the midst of their surrogate ecstasies, that any escape is impossible and that the borderline, or rather the gulf between the two worlds, exists constantly.

To confirm this line of interpretation, it is enough to turn to other poems, in which the lyrical characters' dreams of crossing the border (in both the literal and symbolic senses) seem to have finally come true. The well-known poem "Mona Lisa" (SP 23–25, M 85–87)[13] appears as, first of all, a confrontation between timeless myth and historical experience, and I shall analyze it from this point of view later. However, it is also a poem about a pilgrimage in spatial terms—about the speaker's journey from Poland to Paris and to the legendary painting called by him "Jerusalem in a frame."[14] The present in the poem—the moment when the speaker is finally standing in a room at the Louvre and admiring, or rather forcing himself to admire, La Gioconda—is intertwined with what preceded it, the speaker's reminiscences of his pilgrimage; accordingly, *jestem* in the present tense and *szedłem* in the past tense ("I'm here" and "I kept coming") are the two central words of the poem. The colloquial statement "so I'm here," which recurs time and again as a sort of refrain, initially seems to express the sense of triumph:

> so I'm here
> you see I'm here
>
> I hadn't a hope
> but I'm here

When it returns later, however, it is increasingly marked by the speaker's references to the past—his discreet hints at all the obstacles that had to be overcome ("sometimes it was / sometimes it seemed that / don't even think about it") and at all his friends who had also dreamed about this pilgrimage but did not live long enough to see it happen. The sense of triumph turns gradually into disappointment, as if the speaker asked himself: So I'm here—so what? The confrontation of the old dream with the portrait of a "fat and not too nice signora" brings another disillusionment—an awareness of the discrepancy between the speaker's own experiences and the world of timeless, supra-individual, and abstract cultural values that are totally alien to them (La Gioconda is seen as "hewed off from the meat of life / abducted from home and history"). The poem's conclusion reads as follows:

> between the blackness of her back
> and the first tree of my life
>
> lies a sword
> a melted precipice

The last two lines are a condensation of the basic image of the poem, which dominates it throughout: the image of a separating line, an intraversible border. In the first lines it is a boundary that seems sinister and forbidding owing to both the fairytale-like and the quite literal images of impassable obstacles; however, these borders can still be crossed:

> Through seven mountain frontiers
> barbed wire of rivers
> and executed forests
> and hanged bridges
> I kept coming—

After having reached "Jerusalem in a frame," though, the speaker remains separated, fenced off; he stands "*on a shore* of crimson rope / and eyes,"[15] on the verge of both a spatial and a cognitive "precipice" (Polish *na brzegu* means "on a shore" as well as "on the verge"). The image of a borderline or precipice recurs obsessively in the rest of the poem. Thus, for example, the space "between the second and the right finger / of the right hand" of La Gioconda turns into a "furrow" into which the speaker puts "the empty shells of fates" (of, presumably, his friends who did not live to join him in his pilgrimage: "so I'm here / they were all going to come / I'm alone"). The poem's peculiar optics produce a sense of a precipice even where there can be none according to the laws of physics. While forcing himself to stare into the painting, the speaker experiences characteristic distortions of his own vision—the flat picture becomes, as it were, stereoscopic, and La Gioconda appears "as if constructed out of lenses / concave landscape for a background." Also, particular details of the painting become autonomous and stand out against the background (for instance, La Gioconda's neck and décolletage seem to be "a scarf of glaze" with which she is "smothered"). Thus, there appears an optical motivation for the introduction, in the end, of a startling metaphor that suggests a precipice between La Gioconda's "*back*" and "the first tree of my life" (analogous to the "void" between "her back" and "the first tree of the surroundings," which had been introduced earlier). In the last two lines, "a sword" is not only a possible allusion to the speaker's war experience[16] but, what is more important, is used in its symbolic function known from the legend of Tristan and Yseult: just as the precipice is intraversible, the sword also symbolizes an inviolable prohibition. In the final analysis, there is no contradiction between "I kept coming" and "I'm here": the speaker did not reach his destination and did not achieve his goal. His pilgrimage proved futile and illusionary; his crossing the border, although feasible in a geographic sense, proved unrealizable in a spiritual sense, in the sense of ridding himself of the burden of experience of an Eastern European "barbarian."

The two poems I have analyzed are an apt illustration of the fundamental geographic-cultural paradox in Herbert's work. The world from which his hero has been disinherited, from which he has been separated by one borderline, frontier, precipice, or another, remains a sphere to which he, despite everything, claims his right, for which he yearns, to which he constantly tries to return. At the same time, he is never able to identify with this world fully and effortlessly; the frontier appears impenetrable, disinheritance is an irrevocable fact. Yet the world where the hero belongs, the area of disinheritance, is a realm where he is unable to live in the full sense of the word. It may be—depending on the historical circumstances—a menacing and bloody or merely a gray and stifling world, but it is always a realm from which the hero wants to escape, even though he realizes the utter futility of such dreams. A clear example of this paradox (perhaps even a too transparent one) is provided by Herbert's early poem "The Response" (H 102–103). Its construction might seem arbitrary, but in fact it is based on a simple model, the confrontation of two possibilities. The choice is between two options, metaphorically condensed in the phrases "to spring to one's feet and run . . . to the longed-for other shore" and "to stay here." The additional details make this alternative more geographically specific:

> if our scent hasn't been found by wolves
> and by the man in a sheepskin who cradles
> rapid-fire death on his chest
> we have to spring to our feet and run
> to the applause of dry quick shots
> to the longed-for other shore
>
> . . . . .
>
> but every dream about palm trees
> confirms the choice to stay here

On the one hand, there is a chilly world of wolves and a frontier guard (in the original, the choice of the Russian word *szuba* for his sheepskin, instead of the more Polish and neutral *kożuch,* seems quite deliberate), a world of death, oppression, and terror (the next stanza offers a shudderingly tangible image of a morning visit by the secret police, who make an arrest);[17] on the other, there is a world not only of palm trees with all their cheap exoticism, but also one connected with more fundamental matters. It is, first and foremost, the world that offers access to many different sources of our universal, suprahistorical heritage:

> we bear so many homelands
> on the one earth's one back

Despite this, "the choice to stay here" remains the poem's last word. But it is highly significant that the inaccessible, distant "longed-for other shore" of the wide world has also been associated here with the word "homeland." In other words, instead of opposing "homeland" to "foreign lands," the poem suggests rather the coexistence of "many homelands" for mankind and the "single homeland" for an individual. Even though in "The Response" Herbert opts in an exceptionally unequivocal way for "staying here," in the "single homeland" (which is the destiny of everybody who has shared his nation's experience), he nonetheless also emphasizes the right of an individual to share in the common heritage of mankind despite all borders.

What is particularly important is that Herbert's opting for "staying here" can by no means be interpreted as an idealization of experience that is geographically and nationally confined. His vision of what "staying here" means is devoid of any illusion. The ending of the poem "Prologue" rings a bitter note:

> The ditch where a muddy river flows
> I call the Vistula. It is hard to confess:
> they have sentenced us to such love
> they have pierced us through with such a fatherland
> (N 9, C 22)

Likewise, in the recent poem "Mr. Cogito—the Return," Herbert's hero, deciding to return in spite of the advice of "friends from the better world," knows perfectly well where he returns to and what he loses:

> he sees already
> the frontier
> a plowed field
> murderous shooting towers
> dense thickets of wire
>
> soundless
> armor-plated doors
> slowly close behind him

and already
he is
alone
in the treasure-house
of all misfortunes   (R 20, CR 15)

The opposition of two worlds, divided by frontier or precipice, is not always so dramatically direct in Herbert's poems. In a more complex and, at the same time, less tragic version, the quality of muddiness that characterizes the realm of disinheritance (see "a muddy river" in the above-quoted last stanza of "Prologue") reappears, for instance, in the prose poem "The Homegrown Devil." Here the devil who "came [to Poland] from the West in the beginning of the tenth century" and "initially brimmed over with energy and new ideas," soon degenerated and grew lazy when faced with the "dull virtue" of the folk he was attempting to deprave. "Very soon his sulphurous odor vanished. He acquired the innocent smell of hay. He began to have a little drinking problem. He slackened off completely" (N 33). This humorous poem may seem insignificant, but it complements our model of geographic confrontation with interesting details. The sphere of the lost heritage turns out to have been not so much an idealized Paradise or Arcadia (it was too heavily marked with oppression, cruelty, and absurdity to be called Arcadia, and Herbert is soberly aware of this in many of his poems)[18] as a world whose blessing was that the notions of Paradise and Hell, good and evil, did exist at all. In other words, the heritage is identifiable with the realm of sharply demarcated and defined values; disinheritance is an area in which these values become somewhat "muddy," dimmed, or blurred, a realm where both individuals and nations or civilizations are threatened by "suffocation from formlessness" (R 47, C 71). This extremely important distinction will resurface a number of times throughout our consideration of Herbert's work.

The Past versus the Present

The same kind of ambiguity and paradox as in the case of symbolic West and East marks Herbert's opposition of the past and the present time. Since our access to the past is mostly through cultural artifacts, this opposition naturally often overlaps with another one:

the opposition between cultural myth and immediate experience.[19] There are, however, poems in Herbert's oeuvre in which the stress nonetheless falls positively on the contrast between "in the past" and "today," as if indeed these two time zones had been separated by a "caesura that divided the world's history into a sensible and a senseless part."[20] This is the case, for example, with "Jonah" (SP 40–41, M 94–95), in which the biblical plot, condensed in the initial parts of the poem, is eventually—by the introduction of "the modern Jonah"—reflected upon as an element of the irretrievable past:

> the modern Jonah
> goes down like a stone
> if he comes across a whale
> he hasn't time even to gasp
>
> saved
> he behaves more cleverly
> than his biblical colleague
> the second time he does not take on
> a dangerous mission
> he grows a beard
> and far from the sea
> far from Nineveh
> under an assumed name
> deals in cattle and antiques
>
> agents of Leviathan
> can be bought
> they have no sense of fate
> they are the functionaries of chance
>
> in a neat hospital
> Jonah dies of cancer
> himself not knowing very well
> who he really was

Any attempt to sum up what this poem presents as the nature of the incompatibility between the biblical and the "modern" Jonahs must certainly begin with the opposition of "fate" versus "chance." The past's heritage seems to have been determined by a providential order of things, while the modern disinheritance is a domain of blind chance; today's Jonah might just as well perish without trace as be saved, he might just as well "deal in cattle" as in "antiques" (that is, deal with material goods as well as with culture—both are reduced to commercial merchandise today). Even today's incarnations of Leviathan (presumably, oppressive political systems or institutions) operate through their corrupt agents, "functionaries of chance." Today's Jonah is therefore unable to grasp either the meaning of his existence or the meaning of his death (he dies, significantly, of cancer); consequently, he cannot become a hero of a myth, which would give significance to his experience by sanctifying it or at least preserving it in posterity's collective memory:

> the parable
> applied to his head
> expires
> and the balm of the legend
> does not take to his flesh

An analogical opposition between "the past" and "today" is the semantic axis of the poem "Mr. Cogito's Soul" (R 11–12, CR 6–7). Like the notion of fate in "Jonah," the traditional idea of soul and its relation to body is seen here in the process of disintegration:

> In the past
> we know from history
> she would go out from the body
> when the heart stopped
>
> with the last breath
> she went quickly away
> to the blue meadows of heaven

Whereas today:

> Mr. Cogito's soul
> acts differently
>
> during his life she leaves his body
> without a word of farewell
>
> for months for years she lives
> on different continents
> beyond the frontiers
> of Mr. Cogito
>
> · · · · ·
>
> certainly there are too few souls
> for all humanity

What characterizes the present state of disinheritance is once again the blurring of sharply demarcated borders and the dimming of divisions or oppositions; the traditional dualism of body and soul is dissolved, becoming muddy, indefinable. Such examples as "Jonah" or "Mr. Cogito's Soul" might lead us to think that sometimes at least Herbert does idealize the past without reservation by sketching a conservative utopia of our lost heritage. If even "Jonah" did not seem convincing enough (I shall have more to say about the role of irony in this poem), one would be able to find better examples to support that thesis. It seems obvious, for instance, that in "Why the Classics" (N 51–52, M 137–138) Herbert stands decidedly on the side of Thucydides and the attitude he represented, and against "generals of the most recent wars" who in the case of their defeat "whine on their knees before posterity." Likewise, in the poem "Old Masters" (R 15–16, CR 10–11) his irony, if any, toward the artists of the distant past is mild and tolerant; it is rather admiration and the sense of irreducible distance, which prevail in the poem and find expression in its prayer-like tone:

> The Old Masters
> went without names
>
> . . . . .
>
> they drowned without a trace
> in golden firmaments
> with no cry of fright
> or call to be remembered
>
> the surfaces of their paintings
> are smooth as a mirror
> they aren't mirrors for us
> they are mirrors for the chosen
>
> > I call on you Old Masters
> > in my moments of doubt

This is all true; it is, however, possible to cite a number of other poems in which the past by no means receives unequivocal praise. To quote an example with a theme similar to that of "Old Masters," the prose poem "Martyrdom of Our Lord as Painted by an Anonymous Artist from the Circle of the Rhine Masters" (N 48) shows the personality of another "old master" as something slightly frightening. If his painting is a mirror too, it is a very cold mirror;

the harmonious order of the world as presented by the artist makes any compassion or horror virtually impossible:

> Good artisans are, as we said, nailing Our Lord to
> the cross. Ropes, nails, a stone for grinding the tools,
> are arranged neatly on the sand. There is some bustling
> about, but without excessive nervousness.
> The sand is warm, painted precisely grain by grain.
> Here and there, a little tuft of taut grass and an inno-
> cently white daisy delighting the eye.

The perfection and harmony of the "old" world are marked, then, by the specific ambivalence Herbert's poems always associate with any idea of harmony or perfection. It is an object of nostalgia but is also frightening with its cold inhumanity; an element of the lost heritage, it makes us desire it, but it also makes us even more sure that *today* there is no possible way back to it.

The matter becomes even more complicated when Herbert moves the idea of the past from the sphere of immemorial and remote history (antiquity or the Middle Ages) to that of the most recent past; when he, in other words, confronts "the past" with "the present" within the life of an individual. In such cases, the caesura between the past and the present is usually (although Herbert does not mention the date overtly) 1944, the year when the new order was established, which was at the same time the start of a new disinheritance. This is not a matter of the universal problems of changes in civilization, but rather a specific, personal catastrophe.[21] The "new life" brought by the events of 1944 forces Herbert's hero to throw away his memories of the past, to part company with his old beliefs and loyalties, even to neglect his duty to remember the dead. Reasons of this kind are persuasively presented by the Chorus in "Prologue":

> Throw away memories. Burn remembrance and enter
> the stream of a new life.
> There is only earth. One earth and the seasons of the
> year are over it.

The opposite views are put in the mouth of, significantly, not a collective but an individual speaker (called "He"):

> I flow upstream and they with me
> they look in the eye implacably

> they stubbornly whisper old words
> we eat our bitter bread of despair   (N 8, C 21)

What is contained between "old words" and "a new life" is not only the drama of the Home Army generation, the former fighters against Nazis who, after the war, either fell victim to the Stalinist oppression or had to betray their beliefs in order to survive. It is also a broader and more universal conflict between loyalty to traditional principles and openness to what the new experiences bring. Again, it would be a mistake to maintain that Herbert opts unequivocally for one attitude or another. It is clear that he chooses—I will speak of it in more depth in Chapter 4—*wierność* (faithfulness or loyalty) over forgetfulness, opportunism, and spiritual degradation.[22] One could not, however, say that his faithfulness is uncritical or unaware of its own weaknesses. A few pages after "Prologue," in the same volume, *Napis* [Inscription], is the poem "Awakening," which refers to the same historical threshold of 1944 but places different emphases:

> When the horror subsided the floodlights went out
> we discovered that we were on a rubbish-heap in very
>   strange poses
> some with outstretched necks
> others with open mouths from which still trickled my
>   native land
> still others with fists pressed to eyes
> cramped emphatically pathetically taut
> in our hands we held pieces of sheet iron and bones
> (the floodlights had transformed them into symbols)
> but now they were no more than sheet iron and bones
>
> We had nowhere to go we stayed on the rubbish-heap
> we tidied things up
> the bones and sheet iron we deposited in an archive
>
> We listened to the chirping of streetcars to a swallow-
>   like voice of factories
> and a new life was unrolling at our feet   (N 12, M 132)

The "new life," which appears here as it did in "Prologue," is backed this time by arguments that appeal to reason even more than before. The beginning of the "new life" is after all, shown as a moment of disillusion, an intervention of truth, an empirical realization that heroic symbols are in fact rubbish. Conversely, the war heroes' past is shown as theatrical, staged, a performance with a drop-curtain (in the original, the phrase *opadła groza,* "the horror subsided," is a transformation of *opadła kurtyna,* "the curtain went down"), floodlights, props, grand gestures, and eloquent monologues. All these illusions are unable to persevere when faced with the fact that the world of the past, the world of "old words," was only a useless rubbish-heap. But was it really? Does the implied author of this poem share this presumption fully and without reservation? Note that this poem is not completely unequivocal, either: the sober "tidying things up" appears at the same time as an acceptance of defeat, and in the final sentence "a new life was unrolling at our feet" has a most obviously ironic ring to it. This single metaphor is not enough to make the reader think that the post-1944 "new life" was indeed a sort of red carpet "unrolled" at the feet of the Home Army survivors—a minimum knowledge of postwar history allows one to realize that, this not being the case, the speaker's tone must be bitterly ironic.

Myth versus Experience

The observation of a characteristic relationship between the notion of "the past" and that of "culture" in Herbert's poetry leads us toward the third plane of confrontation between the opposite spheres of heritage and disinheritance. This last type of confrontation is, generally speaking, a cognitive one, since it involves two diametrically different mental approaches to reality, two different sources from which we draw our knowledge of the world and, at the same time, two different purposes for which we use the knowledge we already possess. The simplest way to put this antinomy into words would be to speak of an opposition between cultural messages and sensuous data, or texts and facts; since, however, these cultural messages most often appear in Herbert's poetry as texts with universal and supra-individual meanings and scopes, texts borrowed from, as Northrop Frye would put it, an all-human "grammar of archetypes," I will use the term "myth" to denote all messages of this kind.

Consequently, "myth" will be used in a broad sense, that is, not only as a narrative tale, not only as an extension of ritual, not only as a text rooted in the archaic past. I will be concerned rather with myth in the sense given to it by Ernst Cassirer (in his *Die Philoso-*

phie der symbolischen Formen), that is, myth as one of the symbolic languages, with specific qualities that make it different from, rather than similar to, literature. Myths, as used in Herbert's poems, have a varied ontological status, derive from diverse epochs and cultures, and refer to many different traditions. In this broad sense, myth can appear in these poems—confronted with empirical experience—as a portrait of Mona Lisa, the story of Apollo and Marsyas, the scenery of the Last Judgment, the figure of Hamlet, or the life story of Isadora Duncan; it may be, then, an artifact, a motif from ancient Greek or Roman mythology, or an element of Judaeo-Christian symbolism, as well as a literary character or a historical figure. To avoid engaging in endless discussion over the very definition of "myth,"[23] I shall only observe what all these examples, apparently different from one another in every respect, have in common. Their common denominator is undoubtedly that each of them belongs to the broad repertory of symbols that are universally comprehensible and recognizable in Western civilization today.[24] From this point of view, all these symbols comply with the broadest definition of myth as a method of expressing and organizing the system of beliefs of a given society.

In this same sense, myth is also the direct opposite of a literary work, and it causes confrontation, if not dissonance and conflict, whenever it is incorporated into literature. I am referring here to the well-known antinomy of "Archetype" and "Signature" as proposed by Leslie Fiedler. According to him, the Archetype would mean "any of the immemorial patterns of response to the human situation in its most permanent aspects," while Signature would denote "the sum-total of individuating factors in a work."[25] The confrontation of Archetype and Signature within a literary work is particularly dynamic whenever a work of literature tries to refer to myth or incorporate it. In spite of all analogies between these two "symbolic languages," literature and myth are opposed to each other in several fundamental respects. Myth does not have to be verbalized, while literature is naturally confined to the verbal medium. Myth is a structure that is open to changes, variants, emendations, while a literary work is basically a finished, unchangeable structure. Finally, what is most relevant from the point of view of this discussion of Herbert's work, myth is ahistoric, supra-ethnic, and supra-individual, while a literary work is inevitably determined by its historical and ethnic background and by the personality of its author.

If I might speak of Herbert's particular "mythical method"—as T. S. Eliot spoke of James Joyce's[26]—it would be in the sense that the age-old antinomy of Archetype and Signature is brought by the author of "Elegy of Fortinbras" to its keenest extreme. The element of myth incorporated in Herbert's poems appears as utterly conventionalized, overgrown with popular connotations, reflected in commonplace imagery; this is confronted, in turn, with an utterly individual perspective and vision, which draws from extremely specific experience and is confined to a particular epoch, society, or individual personality. The best possible example here is once again the poem "Mona Lisa." Leonardo's legendary painting is already a myth in its own right; Herbert puts this myth in an additional context of conventional connotations (such as the image of a pilgrimage to the world-famous work of art, and its extraordinary exposition in the scenery of the Louvre) in order to confront it even more dramatically with the perspective of the speaker's extremely individual experience, related to his particular personality, biography, nationality, generational background, and so on. While La Gioconda seems to be "hewed off from the meat of life / abducted from home and history," her observer is anything but an abstraction. The Archetype of popular convictions about the famous painting is thus confronted with the Signature of a lyrical monologue that has strikingly individual features and a personal point of view.

But what is the effect of this confrontation? Just as in the case of the geographic and historical confrontations, here too Herbert seems ambiguous in his valuation of the two opposed poles—at least if we take into account the whole of his work. The critics, whose attention is drawn primarily by the poet's brilliant "demythologizations," do not always realize that there are poems in his oeuvre in which myth triumphs over empirical experience. Let us look first at some of the poems in which Herbert compromises the realm of myth in order to demonstrate its anachronistic uselessness or the dissonance between myth and the historically and geographically defined experience of the individual. I mentioned the Mona Lisa, separated by a "precipice" from the experiences of the speaker, a stranger from twentieth-century Eastern Europe. Analogous meanings are at work in the poem "Our Fear" (SP 34–35, M 90–91), in which the experience of a similar speaker is confronted not so much with a particular artifact as with a more general artistic convention:

Our fear
does not wear a night shirt
does not have owl's eyes
does not lift a casket lid
does not extinguish a candle

does not have a dead man's face either

our fear
is a scrap of paper
found in a pocket
"warn Wójcik
the place on Długa Street is hot"

The presence of myth is revealed indirectly here, through specific props and stylistic allusions that clearly refer to the conventional repertory of a Gothic tale or a horror movie. These pseudo-Romantic accessories are contrasted with the down-to-earthness of specific, contemporary fear, supplied in excess by wars, revolutions, and other by no means mythical pitfalls of history:

our fear
does not rise on the wings of the tempest
does not sit on a church tower
it is down-to-earth
it has the shape
of a bundle made in haste
with warm clothing
provisions
and arms

It would be hard to say that the Gothic convention is compromised here; rather, the poem proves its absolute incommensurability with true horror, the lack of any tangential point between myth and empirical experience.

There are poems of Herbert's in which the pressure of specific, contemporary experience makes his speaker not only question the viability of myth for describing that experience but, more than that, also question myth as such (or at least its traditional formulation). This is the case, for example, in the poem "A Footnote to the Trial" (N 22):

as it seems the entire matter was settled by officials
by pale Pilate and Herod the tetrarch

a faultless administrative procedure
but who can turn it into drama

Hence the scenery of skittish men with beards
and the mob which climbs the hill called
Skull

It could have been gray
devoid of passion

Let us forget for a moment the question of whether this poem's speaker can be considered the author's *porte-parole,* and point out that here the adoption of an extremely empirical point of view strips the traditional version of Pilate's judgment of its dramatic and spectacular qualities. The first part of the poem (omitted in the above quotation) gathers historical and logical arguments that would support the "gray," bureaucratic, and colorless version of the evangelical event. Even more convincingly, this version is also supported by the twentieth-century experience of, to quote Hannah Arendt, "the banality of evil"—an experience that is silently accepted by the poem's speaker as a basic premise of his monologue. Hence the characteristic style of the monologue itself. Such expressions as "it appears improbable that" or "concordance of the opinions of traditional adversaries seems suspicious" could have been used only by someone born in the modern age, a matter-of-fact person who reasons cautiously and in accordance with the premises of experience. The mythical version of the event is accused here of overdramatizing what could have been—as the speaker suggests—just an ordinary show trial, which, as we know well, is usually "gray" and "devoid of passion." Gray—which has exactly the same semantic functions in this poem as "down-to-earth" in "Our Fear"—is, as we shall see often, the color of disinheritance. The silent acceptance of the assumption that a show trial is gray, an element of administrative procedure and therefore normal, says as much about the man disinherited from myth as it does about the myth itself.

If, in the two poems I have just analyzed, the opposition of myth versus experience has much in common with that of past versus present, it does not necessarily mean that this connection is the only possible one. In other words, myth does not have to be viewed only as an element of the irretrievable past from which we have been disinherited by the modern phase of history. Another cross-section of this problem, which does not deal with history, is equally essential in Herbert's poems. Namely, myth can also be questioned from the point of view of experience on the plane of the opposition between the human world and nonhuman nature. Myth, as produced by man, is unable—argues Herbert—to render justice to what does not belong to the human world. That reason alone would be enough to put in doubt, if not to question directly, the supposedly universal and eternal validity of myth. In particular, Herbert's long poem "Study of the Object" is filled with reflections on this problem; an inanimate object—a chair—represents nonhuman nature, which art tries in vain to elevate to the rank of myth.[27]

Even though Herbert can by no means be counted among those poets who rashly condemn culture as a whole,[28] it is a fact that, in his poetic world, myth is definitely not a key to every mystery of the universe. But empirical experience is not that key, either. The world we approach through the senses seems tangible and stable, but in fact it does not admit human consciousness; a pebble can be taken in a human hand but it "cannot be tamed" (SP 59, M 108), a wooden die can be cut in two, but "immediately its inside becomes a wall and there occurs the lightning-swift transformation of a mystery into a skin" (SP 71, M 116). Just as with the geographical and historical oppositions, the confrontation of myth and empirical experience is not concluded with an unequivocal, final settlement. The "face" of these poems' implied author is—like the face of his persona, Mr. Cogito, in one of the poems (P 5–6)—a biological legacy from his human and prehuman ancestors as well as the cultural heritage of thousands of years of civilization.[29]

THUS far, in this investigation of Herbert's incessant confrontation of the realms of heritage and disinheritance, I have discussed poems in which that confrontation is relatively direct, through overt references to the notions of—to use a form of shorthand—the West, the past, and myth on the one hand, and the East, modern times, and empirical experience on the other. Now it is time to characterize Herbert's more indirect methods of confrontation—methods that resort to poetic devices based on symbolic structures of meaning. Specifically, I will examine the antinomic semantic patterns that appear on three levels of this poetry—briefly and imprecisely speaking, in its imagery, in its system of values, and in its world of

characters. More precisely, I will be dealing with Herbert's antinomies as presented by his symbolic key words, his aesthetic and
ethical categories, and the literary personages he employs.

Imagery

It is impossible not to begin by observing that yet another oversimplification in a typical reading of Herbert's poetry results from the
critic's focusing his attention on its higher semantic levels. The critics usually appear to take into consideration, as it were, only the
meanings of Herbert's *sentences* and their configurations, while
treating the lesser semantic units as if they did not matter at all. In
fact, however, Herbert's poetry also reveals its precise inner organization on its lower levels; his *words* are burdened with meaning
and only seem to be transparent and unequivocal. I will not try to
determine whether this inner semantic organization on the level of
individual words is deliberately planned or the result of unconscious obsessions. In any case, it is a fact that the role played in
Herbert's poetry by symbolic key words (and also by metaphors,
which will be the subject of the next chapter) is enormous and is
underestimated by critics. By key words I mean particular words
Herbert uses with characteristic frequency—words rich with symbolic meanings and, in full accordance with the antinomic nature
of this poetry, arranged in bilateral sets of opposites. At least three
such recurring pairs of key words strike Herbert's reader.

White—Gray

Contrary to the usual comments about its "intellectual" character,
Herbert's imagery is clearly sensual: its central categories relate to
sight and touch. Herbert's visual imagery, however, is dominated
not as much by contrasting colors as by the opposition of whiteness
and grayness[30] (with an analogy in the opposition of light and
shadow, to be analyzed next). As in ancient sculptures or temples
(or, rather, in what remains of them),[31] all the infinite spectrum of
color is virtually reduced to the simple contrast of white and gray.

If we try, however, to examine the specific contexts in which
whiteness or white appears in Herbert's poetry, the overall sense of
this word proves to far exceed the range of color-related or visual
meanings. The first use of the word "white" in Herbert's first vol-

ume already puts us on an interesting track: the title of the poem "White Eyes" (SS 14) refers to the eyes of a dead man; the poem depicts someone in his death throes. Another poem from the same collection, "To Apollo," is based on analogical associations:

> listening intently to his own song
> he raised his lyre to the height of silence
>
> gazing into himself
> his eyes white as a stream   (SS 21)

The eyes in marble statues are, quite literally, white, and because Herbert mentions this whiteness, Apollo must be perceived as a statue and not as a living god; even though the poem addresses him directly, the god appears invariably in the context of such words or expressions as "silence," "silent" ("Give me back my hope / o silent white head," SS 22), "gazing into himself," and so on.

What is "white," then, is the eyes of the dead and marble statues; white is the color of death and silence. Let me quote a handful of examples from other poems:

> One must dig in warm leaves with living hands for a
>   long time
> one must trample images
> call the sunset a phenomenon
> in order to discover beneath all this
> a dead white
> philosophers' stone   ("The Cultivation of Philosophy," SS 54)
>
> but there is no voice
> only the senile garrulity of water
> salty nothing
> a white bird's wing
> stuck dry to a stone   ("Voice," H 17, M 40)
>
> then grows in me
> not fear not love
> but white stone
>
> . . . . .
> deeper than the blood of the earth
> more luxuriant than a tree
> is the white stone
> indifferent fullness   ("White Stone," H 45–46, C 6)

> happily I will give my color of eyes
> pattern of nails and curve of eyelids
> I the perfectly objective
> made from white crystals of anatomy
> ("To My Bones," SP 68, M 115)

> what was our death at the beginning:
> a helpless white ant egg   ("An Ordinary Death," N 18)

> Once there was breath on window-panes here, the
> smell of a roast, the same face in the mirror. Now
> there is a museum . . . Between his closet, his bed, and
> his table—a white border of absence, strict like the cast
> of a hand.   ("The House of the Poet," N 29)

> Three-dimensional illustrations from deplorable
> textbooks. Deathly white with dry hair, an empty
> quiver, and a wilted thyrsus. They stand immobile on
> barren islands, among the living stones, under a leafy
> sky. Symmetrical Aphrodite, Jove mourned by his
> dogs, Bacchus drunk with plaster.
> ("Ornamental yet True," N 34, C 16)

> The poet in his menopause
> . . . . .
> against the background of young blue
> the white tree of his veins
> ("Mr. Cogito and the Poet of Certain Age," P 41, 44)

> and also white gallows because the dry pods of bodies
> hang from them   ("A Landscape," *Twórczość* 1979:10)

Just as often, whiteness is not mentioned directly but appears as
an obvious attribute of materials or substances such as plaster,
snow, or lime. Regardless of its direct or indirect presence, however, whiteness is placed, as a rule, in certain stable contexts. It
appears accompanied by stone, plaster, lime, bones (this is the sense
of the "white crystals of anatomy" as quoted above), or bird feath-
ers. Also by paper; the expression "a white sheet of paper" seems
to be ametaphoric and prosaic, yet in two poems in which it appears the paper's whiteness has also a symbolic sense—it denotes a
"pure" but, at the same time, dead literature (or its critical dissec-

tion) as contrasted with "dirty" but genuine spheres of experience or the reader's spontaneous reaction (the use of the word *ziemia,* "earth" or "soil," is significant in both cases):

> in the white margins
> the prints of fingers and the soil
> have marked with rough thumb-nail
> rapture and condemnation
>> ("Journey to Kraków," H 24, M 43)

> A blonde girl is bent over a poem. With a pencil
> sharp as a lancet she transfers the words to a blank
> page ["a white page" in the original] and changes them
> into strokes, accents, caesuras. The lament of a fallen
> poet now looks like a salamander eaten away by ants.
> When we carried him away under machine-gun fire,
> I believed that his still warm body would be resur-
> rected in the word. Now as I watch the death of the
> words, I know there is no limit to decay. All that will
> be left after us in the black earth will be scattered syl-
> lables. Accents over nothingness and dust.
>> ("Episode in a Library," H 119, M 64)

White also tends to appear accompanied by characteristic sensual qualities: brightness or clarity but also dryness. In a more abstract sense, another context for white is usually lifelessness, indifference, barrenness, solitude, absence, silence, or blindness (compare the blind eyes of ancient statues, "eyes blinded with lime," SP 15, or even "the astronauts' white cane," SP 49, M 101), although these qualities can shift semantically toward perfection, objectivity, symmetry, or fullness. This perfection and fullness can be sneered at or ironically compromised (in "To My Bones" we find an apostrophe to the speaker's own skeleton: "you my little monument not quite complete," M 115), but whiteness is in fact an ambivalent symbol. It is all colors at once, but also none; it means fullness but also absence, perfection but also lifelessness.[32]

Thus, it seems striking that within Herbert's antinomic symbolism the opposite of "white" is not so much "black" or any color as "gray." A color on the one hand and blackness on the other can even function as paradoxical synonyms for whiteness, depending on whether its meaning is closer to "fullness" or to "absence." The poem "A Knocker," for instance, reads as follows:

> There are those who grow
> gardens in their heads
> paths lead from their hair
> to sunny and white cities
>
> . . . . .
>
> for others the green bell of a tree
> the blue bell of water   (H 32–33, M 45)

Here white has the same value as green and blue as a symbol of liberated fullness, which is the principal quality of "others'" (that is, other poets') imagination. At the opposite extreme, in the poem "A Black Rose" (SP 15) the rose of the title "emerges / black / from the eyes blinded / with lime" and every color, including white, can be derived from it. Likewise, the metaphor "a black drop of infinity" used in "Revelation" (SP 65, M 112) leads us to an important identification: infinity is actually a synonym for nothingness, the perfect fullness of "white" is only the negative of perfect absence as symbolized by "black."

The truly essential opposition, then, can rather be observed between "white" and "gray." Let us gather a few examples again:

> on the street of festive processions
> the gray prison wall is an eye sore
> an ugly stain on an ideal landscape
>   ("The Ornament-Makers," H 88)
>
> a barge flows down the river window-panes tremble
>   and wail
> the stucco shapes a gray wreath on the pavement
> the hair of the dust stretch almost to infinity
>   ("A Farewell to the City," N 16)
>
> It could have been gray
> devoid of passion   ("A Foot-Note to the Trial," N 22)
>
> most of them
> stand motionless
> in the middle of a dull landscape
> of ashy hills ["gray hills" in the original]
> parched trees
>   ("Mr. Cogito and the Movement of Thoughts," P 24, C 41)

The function of grayness is particularly evident in the poem "Nike Who Hesitates," where it is contrasted with whiteness even though the latter is not mentioned overtly (since we naturally imagine Nike as a marble statue, such a direct mention is unnecessary):

> Nike is most beautiful at the moment
> when she hesitates
>
> . . . . .
>
> For she sees
> a solitary youth
> he goes down the long tracks
> of a war chariot
> on a gray road in a gray landscape
> of rocks and scattered juniper bushes   (SS 74, M 27)

There are also cases in which it is grayness that is not mentioned directly, although the context indicates clearly that "gray" is what is meant. "The Hair," for instance, in the poem of that same title (SP 30, M 88) is:

> not white
> not black
> rather their color is
> rustle

In yet other cases, the visual impression of grayness can be evoked by means of metonymical association with a specific substance or object: dust, ash (N 26), clay, old stucco, dirt (P 26). As I have already mentioned, grayness is an attribute of disinheritance. Grayness is a dominant feature in the human world as opposed to that of the gods (see "Nike Who Hesitates"), in the world of barbarians as opposed to that of the ancient traditions (compare "The Longobards," N 26, M 127), in empirical reality as opposed to myth ("The Ornament-Makers"). In regard to the latter, the prose poem "Małachowski's Ravine" (N 30) offers an especially interesting example of complex symbolic connotations in the use of color (or its absence, for that matter). An episode from the Napoleonic wars is first presented almost as a colorful nineteenth-century lithograph. The "blue and amaranth-purple" Polish commander with a "golden moustache" leads his soldiers from a "shadowy ravine" up, "toward the sun's glory," toward brightness and whiteness. When a skirmish with the Russians begins, the officer's defeat and death are metaphorically equated with his fall through "cloudy" grayness into blackness ("his aiguillettes turn black"). At the same time, this is a downfall from the heights of myth into the abyss of the particular, from the past into the present, where the only sign in remembrance of these colorful soldiers is a "gray" memorial stone.

Light—Shadow

"Małachowski's Ravine" is also a good example of how another important pair of symbolic key words adds complementary meanings to those implied by "white" and "gray." This opposition is between "light" and "shadow" (not surprisingly, on this plane "darkness" performs functions analogous to those of "black" in the previous one).[33] Beginning with the very title of Herbert's first collection, *Chord of Light,* (which, incidentally, connects two of Apollo's traditional attributes—the lyre and light), the notion of light is always close to heritage, classical tradition, Mediterranean past.[34] *Lucidus ordo* (*Barbarian in the Garden,* 153) is synonymous with the lost harmony. From this point of view, the arrangement of metaphorical meanings in the initial part of "To Marcus Aurelius" seems significant:

> Good night Marcus put out the light
> and shut the book For overhead
> is raised a gold alarm of stars
> heaven is talking some foreign tongue
> this the barbarian cry of fear
> your Latin cannot understand
> Terror continuous dark terror
> against the fragile human land
>
> begins to beat It's winning (SS 29, M 22)

On the one hand there is Marcus Aurelius's lamp (thus in the original), on the other the "dark," even though star-lit, sky of barbarity. This simple opposition grows much more complicated in some other poems:

> Birds leave
> their shadows in nests
>
> so leave your lamp
> instrument and book
>
> let us come to the hill
> where the air grows

> I will point my finger
> at the absent star
>
> . . . . .
>
> maybe glimmers will descend
> along our bent backs
>
>> Indeed indeed I tell you
>> great is the gulf
>> between us
>> and light   ("The Chord," SS 41–42)

The nature of light is not uniform, then: the light of a "lamp" proves insufficient, since its source is, like an "instrument" or a "book," an artificial creation of man. That kind of light can be actually equated to "shadow"; the true light radiates from a star, but it is separated from people by a "gulf" or "precipice" (Polish *przepaść* means both). Pure light is synonymous with perfection and fullness, two unattainable qualities; all-encompassing, it, like "whiteness" and "blackness," is an abstraction, a nothing (hence "the *absent* star" in this poem or the "black light" in another, SS 49). And thus, Herbert defines light as the absence of an object:

> The most beautiful is the object
> which does not exist
>
> . . . . .
>
> the hairs
> of all its lines
> join
> in one stream of light   ("Study of the Object," SP 54, M 104)

This absence can be symbolized by light as well as by darkness or blackness:

> mark the place
> where stood the object
> which does not exist
> with a black square   (ibid. SP 55, M 105)

Similarly, in the poem "Path" (N 17, C 13), to which I shall return soon, Herbert practically equates "dark alchemy" with "too clear an abstraction"—neither of the two is able to reflect the "multiplicity" of the world. One can assume that the true image of multiplicity would be only shadow, semidarkness, chiaroscuro. Such a supposition is voiced in a relatively transparent way in the poem

"Daedalus and Icarus" (SS 78–79), whose semantic axis is the opposition of earth and sky, shadow and light.[35] Here Daedalus represents the striving for the light, which could be fully satisfied only by a near-impossible surmounting of human limitations; in contrast, Icarus is a representative of the human condition, which naturally gravitates toward the earth and shadow—he is "all immersed in the earth's dark rays." Herbert's Icarus, in keeping with the myth, finally falls (as in Brueghel's well-known painting or W. H. Auden's "Musée des Beaux Arts": "the last image left after him is the sight of a childishly small heel / which is swallowed by the voracious sea"); it is, however, significant that the final "Commentary" declares both partners of the previous dialogue to be equally right—or rather, equally wrong.

Air—Earth

The examples of "Path" and "Daedalus and Icarus" have drawn our attention to another pair of symbolic key words. These are the names of the elements, which appear frequently in Herbert's poetry and always carry special significance. We can say that "air" is, as a rule, equivalent to "whiteness" and "light," while "earth" (often appearing in more specific form, such as "clay") is usually linked with "gray" and "shadow." "Water," which is also frequently used, has a function analogous to that of "blackness" and "dark"—it seems to be the exact opposite of "air" (if only for the strongly pronounced contrast in their sensual qualities, dryness versus wetness), but, in fact, it is only its negative copy. If in certain poems (such as "To the River," R 14, CR 9) water appears as synonymous with the primordial life, substantiality, and empirical experience, and thus offers an alternative to the dry, evasive, and imperceptible air, in certain others it is semantically equated with death (Icarus perishes in the sea), absence, silence. This is particularly clear in "Path,"[36] where the choice—presented in a slightly allegorical way, to be sure—between two paths, one leading to a spring, the other to the top of a hill (in other words, one to the water, the other toward the air), ends in a disappointment: one choice is "dark alchemy," the other "too clear an abstraction." Characteristically enough, the spring is associated not only with qualities such as "humidity" but also with "darkness" and tangibility (compare "touch"):

if you chose the spring you went through steps of half-
   light
touch led blindly into deeper and deeper darkness
to the mother of elements honored by Thales
in order to unite finally with the humid heart of things
with the dark grain of cause   (N 17, C 13)

The relationships among the earth, water, and air are demonstrated even more precisely by the poem "Island" (N 10, C 3):

There is a sudden island Sculpture of the sea cradle
graves between ether and salt
the smokes of its paths wind around rocks
and the raising of voices above drone and silence
Here seasons parts of the world have a home
and shadow is good good night and good sun
the ocean would be glad to leave its bones here
leaves bandage the tired shoulder of the sky
Its fragility among the screams of the elements
when at night human fire talks in the mountains
and at daybreak before dawn sparkles
first the light of the springs rises in the ferns

Bypassing the interesting semantic interplay of the notions of light
and dark, let us note only that the island is located between "ether"
and "salt," that is, between the sky and the ocean, air and water; it
is also "the raising of voices" both above the "drone" of the sea and
above the "silence" of the sky. "Drone" and "silence" are, in fact,
the same: they do not say anything or mean anything. For that
reason, the poem suggests a stronger relation between the sky and
the ocean than between either of these two and the island—the
earth becomes the opposite extreme of both air and water.

Patterns of this sort in Herbert's poetry are not always as consistent as they are in "Island"—after all, poetry is not a mathemat-
ical equation. In the early poem "The Last Will," for instance, water
is depicted as a kind of go-between for the other elements (it "cir-
culates between the earth and sky," SS 46). Usually, however, the
opposition between the earth and the air carries the same meanings
and is put in the same contexts. Let us note the characteristic semantic environment of the word "air" in the following fragments:

[Nike's] right hand beautiful as a command
rests against the air   ("Nike Who Hesitates," SS 74, M 27)

> This was the most beautiful blue of my life: dry,
> hard, and breath-takingly pure. The enormous angels
> of air were going slowly out of it.
> ("A Nail in the Sky," SP 70)

> so at last it would become sober in the air dried by
> thunder   ("Sense of Identity," P 13, C 37)

In the poem "Descent" (N 11), the morning is metaphorically defined as "a bell of air" and compared to an angel descending from the sky. These few examples suffice to demonstrate how persistently the same associations recur in Herbert's poetry. The attribute of air, which often appears in the metaphorical company of angels or ancient gods, is always brightness, dryness, purity, identical with perfection but also having something to do with death. On the contrary, earth, as a rule, appears in a context of shadow, grayness, humidity (if it is dry, it's the dirty dryness of dust), while at the same time synonymous with life, imperfect but tangible and real:

> Finally us with an iridescent lump of earth under our
> eyelids
> . . . . . .
> only we shall meet a horrible fate
> flame and lamentation
> because baptized by the earth
> we were too dauntless in our uncertainty
> ("Baptism," H 8)

It is significant that here, as with the two previous antinomies, neither of the opposites is granted clear superiority or victory. The sensual opposition of dryness versus humidity, for instance, is undoubtedly crucial for the "air—earth" relationship, but it seems to be quite ambivalent. In the above-quoted "Sense of Identity," a stone, with which the lyrical persona tries to identify, is alternately soaked by rain (and this "clash of elements . . . the loss of one's own nature" is "both beautiful and humiliating") and drying out (becoming "sober") in the "air dried by thunder." In "A Knocker" (H 33, M 45), "dryness" is meant as a limitation (that is, a limitation of the speaker's imagination as compared with the imagination of those whose "schools of images / stream down from their foreheads"), but also a strength; that imagination, compared to a piece of board struck with a wooden stick,

prompts me
with the moralist's dry poem

yes—yes
no—no

System of Values

What I have said about the essentially antinomical structure of Herbert's poetic world also pertains to the values he refers to, or, more precisely, his ethical or aesthetic categories. They too are arranged in antinomic pairs, each of which is characterized by its ambivalence: within the whole of Herbert's poetry any confrontation remains basically unresolved; neither of the opposite notions can be marked with a stable and unquestionable plus or minus sign.

The Abstract— The Tangible

Despite everything that is usually said about Herbert by his critics, this kind of ambivalence is also noticeable in his frequently used categories of the abstract and the tangible.[37] True, if we were to be influenced by overt declarations of the poet himself (who, in one of his poems, admits his "rapacious love of the concrete," R 25, CR 20), and especially if we were to concentrate on the early stage of his career, we could easily assume that Herbert is a programmatic defender of the concrete against abstraction,[38] a materialistic empiricist or even "reist." This could be documented in those of his poems which can be read almost as miniature treatises on gnoseology. The poem "The Troubles of a Little Creator" (SS 58–60), for instance, contains a manifesto of such extreme empiricism that it denies the very feasibility of communicating one's experience; according to the poem, a sensual experience remains the exclusive property of the individual, who, as it were, creates the world anew with each specific act of perception:

> You won't pass on your knowledge to anyone
> your hearing and touch are only yours
> everyone must create anew
> his infinity and his beginning

Things, however, grow more complicated, even within the same poem:

If you trust your five senses
the world will contract into a hazelnut

If you believe in your rushing thoughts
you will go far into unfailing darkness
on the great stilts of telescopes

This precisely may be your fate
to be a creature with no ready-made shapes
who experiences and forgets

Both extreme sensual empiricism and cerebral speculation prove fallible: while the former reduces the world to a testable but limited size, the latter dissolves it in unascertainable darkness. As the last of the above-quoted stanzas suggests, the truth lies somewhere in between, in an open attitude that rejects "ready-made shapes" (recall a similar expression in another poem: "an exile of obvious shapes"). In another poetic manifesto of gnoseology, "The Touch" (H 12–13), we encounter a different sort of complication. Here the very notion of sensual experience appears too broad from the point of view of the requirements of extreme empiricism. Nearly all the senses disappoint the speaker with their fallibility and deceptiveness; the only exception is touch:

and then comes unfailing touch
it restores immobility to things
the dam of ten fingers rises
over the ears' lies and the eyes' confusion
hard distrust and disbelief
put fingers into the world's wound
and separate the thing from what it seems to be

The last three lines, which suggest an analogy between the act of cognition and the deed of doubting Thomas,[39] imply more complex meanings. Thomas was indeed a skeptical empiricist, but he could also have been defined as faint-hearted. Therefore, "separating things from what they seem to be" is not necessarily an infallible method for reaching the ultimate truth about reality. The poem ends with a meaningful statement: "the touch grows on the edge of the truth." The tangible concrete is, then, only one "edge" or fringe of the truth; touch is closer to truth than the other senses, but is still unable to reach its inner core.[40]

Critical oversimplifications concerning Herbert's allegedly absolute empiricism are particularly easy to unmask with a close reading of those of his poems which are often cited as being programmatically "reistic" and are compared to the work of Francis Ponge or, in Polish poetry, the early work of Miron Białoszewski.[41] I have in mind those poems or prose poems in which the central object of description is a single material object: "Stool" (SS 63, M 24), "Pebble" (SP 59, M 108), "Wooden Die" (SP 71, M 116). Among these three, "Stool" is indeed perhaps the most "reistic" and empirical of Herbert's poems. What is also significant about it is that history appears here as a key to philosophy—the speaker's trust in the tangible concrete is the reverse side of his distrust in ideological "charlatans," his cognitive reductionism is the natural result of his aversion to the utter relativism of Marxist dialectics:[42]

> —Do you know my darling they were charlatans
> who said: the hand lies the eye
> lies when it touches shapes that are empty—
>
> they were bad people envious of things
> they wanted to trap the world with the bait of denial
>
> how to express to you my gratitude wonder
> you come always to the call of the eye
> with great immobility explaining by dumb-signs
> to a sorry intellect: we are genuine—
> At last the fidelity of things opens our eyes

This is, incidentally, the same kind of protest against twisted justifications of brute force and lie, which years later would reappear in the following characterization of Mr. Cogito's logic:

> he adored tautologies
> explanations *idem per idem*
>
> that a bird is a bird
> slavery means slavery
> a knife is a knife
> death remains death
>
> he loved
> the flat horizon
> a straight line
> the gravity of the earth
> ("Mr. Cogito and the Imagination," R 22–23, CR 17)

"Wooden Die" and "Pebble," however, can by no means be interpreted as manifestations of trust in the "fidelity of things" and the "genuineness" of the tangible concrete. The cognitive credo expressed in "Stool" is complemented by "Wooden Die" with an essential complication. Here we have an opposition between the outer shape or appearance of an object and its inner "essence"; the former accessible through the senses, while the latter is out of their reach:

> A wooden die can be described only from without.
> We are therefore condemned to eternal ignorance of its
> essence. Even if it is quickly cut in two, immediately
> its inside becomes a wall and there occurs the light-
> ning-swift transformation of a mystery into a skin.
>
> For this reason it is impossible to lay foundations for
> the psychology of a stone ball, of an iron bar, of a
> wooden cube.

The last sentence is particularly meaningful here: contrary to "Stool" and its quite simple-hearted belief in the chance of cognitive communication between a human being and an inanimate object,[43] this poem emphasizes precisely the intraversibility of the border between humans and things. Similar conclusions are drawn by "Pebble," in which, however, the emphases are distributed in a slightly different manner. What is most exposed here is the "perfection" of things as opposed to the imperfection of humans (for that reason I shall postpone the analysis of this poem for a moment). Finally, an interesting addition to the cognitive skepticism of "Wooden Die" is offered by the poem "Rosy Ear" (H 68–69, M 53–54), which explores the same problem, our "eternal ignorance" of the "essence" of things, while speaking, in fact, not about an inanimate thing but about a person, one close to the speaker's heart. The speaker, who is convinced that he "knows" his long-time lover "so well," happens to focus his gaze on her ear, which "in the lamplight / falling from behind us" appears to him as "a comic petal of skin / a conch with living blood / inside it":

> I didn't say anything then—
>
> it would be good to write
> a poem about a rosy ear
> but not so that people would say
> what a subject he chose
> he's trying to be eccentric

so that nobody would even smile
so that they would understand that I proclaim
a mystery

I didn't say anything then
but that night when we were in bed together
delicately I essayed
the exotic taste
of a rosy ear

Let us note some interesting analogies to "Wooden Die." The reason why the ear seems to be a fascinating "mystery" (in other words, why it seems to reveal the "essence" of the lover) is that against the lamplight one can see what is "inside it." Even if we assume that this is not an illusion (contrary to "Wooden Die," this poem is far from unequivocal skepticism), the "mystery" appears to be accessible only to the speaker's senses (characteristically, he is able only to "essay" its "taste"). It cannot, however, be communicated to others; as soon as the speaker decides to do so, he immediately imagines the skeptical reactions of his audience, and the final outcome of his hesitation is self-ironic—his poem about the ear pretends, as it were, that it has not been written at all. The limitations of sensual empiricism are fully revealed here. Even though the sensual experience is able to reach "the edge of the truth," it remains incommunicable to others and is the sole property of the person who experiences it. Likewise, in the poem "Attempt at a Description" (SP 52–53, M 103) an attempt at the safest description possible—that of one's own body—also ends in failure. It begins with a characteristic vacillation, as if the speaker were not quite decided as to the most specific and concrete object for him to describe:

First I will describe myself
starting from my head
or better from my foot
or from my hand
from the little finger of my left hand

But even such utter cognitive cautiousness proves to be of no avail. The poem's conclusion is that reducing a description to one's own physical qualities may be the safest method possible, but that it too is restricted to the individual's experience, which cannot be transmitted to others. Any "agreement" (*porozumienie,* meaning also "understanding" and "communication") between an individual and others comes down to the "tautology" of their belonging to the same human species:

> it is a peculiar finger
> a left hand's little finger unique in the whole world
> given to me directly
>
> other little fingers of a left hand
> are a cold abstraction
> with mine
> we have a common date of birth
> date of death
> a common loneliness
>
> only blood
> busy with scansion of dark tautologies
> binds together distant shores
> with a thread of mutual agreement

The extreme of "touch," pure sensualism, is finally rejected. But the extreme of pure abstraction is also rejected. "The absolute" is unattainable whenever one is dealing with the "clay" of the specifically human, the human body or senses, the uniqueness of human personality. The ironic poem "Report from Paradise" (N 25, M 131) indicates that this remains a guiding principle even in the sphere where only the pure spirituality would seem to exist:

> At first it was to have been different
> luminous circles choirs and degrees of abstraction
> but they were not able to separate exactly
> the soul from the flesh and so it would come here
> with a drop of fat a thread of muscle
> it was necessary to face the consequences
> to mix a grain of the absolute with a grain of clay

A similar vision is evoked by the poem "Eschatological Forebodings of Mr. Cogito," in which the lyrical persona's apprehension consists in his fear that the "recruiting commission" to Paradise will demand that he rid himself of "earthly habits" and the "vestiges of the senses." Mr. Cogito would even be ready to renounce his senses of smell, taste, and hearing:

> he will only
> explain to the severe angels

that the sense of sight and of touch
don't want to leave him

. . . . .

he will yield to all tortures
gentle persuasions
but to the end he will defend
the magnificent sensation of pain

and a few weathered images
on the bottom of the burnt-out eye   (R 34–36, CR 29–31)

The Perfect—The Erroneous

The question is: why does Mr. Cogito try so stubbornly to "convince the angels / he is incapable / of heavenly / service"? We encounter here the opposition between angels and humans, which (as we shall see) plays a central role in Herbert's world of literary characters; on the level of values, however, the same kind of opposition is represented by the antinomy of perfection and error.[44] In the poem "In a Studio" (SP 11), divine perfection appears as, in fact, an inhumane quality;[45] the imperfection of a human being—"a little Creator," as another poem puts it—is "good," consistent with life and conducive to life:

> When building the world our Lord
> wrinkled his brow
> calculating calculating calculating
> that's why the world is perfect
> and uninhabitable
>
> on the other hand
> the world of the painter
> is good
> and full of mistakes

Moreover, the last lines of this poem depict the painter as "*correcting the world*" with his "*unconscious hand*"—his human errors rectify, then, the greater error that would be, paradoxically, a world of inhuman perfection.

Man's imperfection singles him out, however, not only as an exile from the Paradise of God and angels but also as an outcast from the garden of nature. Compared to him, inanimate elements of nature are also perfect. The poem "Pebble," (SP 59, M 108) which elaborates this idea most clearly, must be quoted in full here:

> The pebble
> is a perfect creature
>
> equal to itself
> mindful of its limits
>
> filled exactly
> with a pebbly meaning
>
> with a scent which does not remind one of anything
> does not frighten anything away does not arouse desire
>
> its ardour and coldness
> are just and full of dignity
>
> I feel a heavy remorse
> when I hold it in my hand
> and its noble body
> is permeated by a false warmth
>
> —Pebbles cannot be tamed
> to the end they will look at us
> with a calm and very clear eye

Is this poem a "reistic" praise of the superiority of things over humans, evidence—as more than one critic would have it—of Herbert's "cult of perfect, closed things, the cult of the stoicism of inanimate objects"?[46] Yes and no. If we read the text closely, its meaning appears ambivalent. The semantic peculiarity of this finely wrought poem is that even though it includes no mention (apart from the single pronoun "us" in the last stanza) of the human world, each statement concerning the pebble is supposed to be read, as if in a negative reflection, as a statement on the human condition. As opposed to inanimate objects—we read—man is imperfect, he constantly trespasses his natural limits, gropes blindly for the meaning of his existence, is full of chaotic fears and desires, risks errors and humiliations, is often base or deceitful. Nevertheless, the ending discreetly introduces a contrasting tone; the apparent admiration for the object's perfection conceals, in fact, the speaker's horror at its indifference to human suffering, loneliness, and death ("the end"). The "perfection," "calm" and "clarity" of the pebble perhaps, then, result only from its being *poorer* than man—from its being unable to suffer, die, or experience "the magnificent feeling of pain" mentioned in "Eschatological Forebodings of Mr. Cogito." If anything makes the world of things closer to man than the world of angels, it is only the fact that things are material—and, therefore, both accessible (at least on their surface) to our senses and not completely devoid of flaws, "mistakes," and imperfection. For this reason, in the prose poem "Anything Rather than an Angel" (SP 78, M 119) the speaker prefers, as if it were a lesser evil, incarnation as an inanimate object rather than as an angel (also worth noting here are the characteristic attributes of heaven— dryness, brightness, "airiness," and abstraction):

> If after our death they want to transform us into a
> tiny withered flame that walks along the paths of
> winds—we have to rebel. What good is an eternal lei-
> sure on the bosom of air, in the shade of a yellow halo,
> amid the murmur of two-dimensional choirs?
>   One should enter rock, wood, water, and cracks of a
> gate. Better to be the creaking of a floor than shrilly
> transparent perfection.

The idea of human imperfection therefore naturally parallels the function performed by the notion of the tangible concrete in the previous pair of opposites.[47] Sometimes both pairs of opposed categories engage in more complex interrelations. The anecdotal prose poem "Mr. Cogito and the Pearl" (P 12), for instance, is a recollection of Mr. Cogito's "youthful march toward perfection": one day he decided to realize the slogan *"per aspera ad astra"* by not removing a pebble that was hurting him from his shoe. This "heroic solution" made it, however, impossible for Mr. Cogito to listen attentively to a lecture about "the concept of the idea in Plato," since he was being tormented by pain from his bruised heel. As we see, suffering—shown here, as opposed to in "Eschatological Forebodings" or "Pebble," in a slightly caricatured and self-ironic way—can at first seem a path toward perfection, but its carnal and trivial concreteness prevents the hero from achieving his pure and abstract goal.

Analogously, the concreteness and erratic unpredictability of life collide with the perfection of a mystical revelation in two thematically connected poems: "Revelation" (SP 64–65, M 111–112) and "Mr. Cogito and Pure Thought" (P 20–21). In both poems, there is an ironic unmasking of the ideal of perfection (identified with "immobility" and "emptiness"), which allegedly can be reached through mystical detachment from life's trivialities and through a state of "pure" illumination. In the former poem, the speaker has almost succeeded in accomplishing that ("my immobility / was nearly perfect"), when suddenly:

> the postman rang
> I had to pour out the dirty water
> prepare tea
>
> Siva lifted his finger
> the furniture of heaven and earth
> started to spin again
>
> I returned to my room
> where is that perfect peace
> the idea of a glass
> was being spilled all over the table

In the final part of the poem, the speaker promises himself not to let himself be roused from his state of "revelation" anymore and to continue to keep his eyes

> fixed
> upon the heart of things
>
> a dead star
>
> a black drop of infinity

The very choice of epithets, however, reveals the self-ironic implied meaning of this passage: perfection is, in fact, identical with life-lessness; purity equals nothingness.[48] Similarly, in the other of the two poems, Mr. Cogito appears unable to attain the ideal of "pure thought," because he is distracted by the sensual concrete that cannot be ousted even from the most abstract reasoning:

> he wasn't able to tear
> his inner eye
> from the mailbox
> the smell of the sea was in his nostrils
> crickets tickled his ear
> and beneath a rib he felt the fingers of her absence

Again, in the final part the hero can only hope that

> some time later . . .
> he will attain the state of satori
> and will be

> as the masters instruct
> empty and
> astonishing

The words "some time later" are made more precise by a sober explanation: "when he cools off." Perfection turns out once again to be synonymous with death. But what Herbert means here is a passive, regressive, mystical, or Buddhist idea of perfection; as we will see later, he by no means rejects the idea of an active striving for perfection, despite all the irony it often provokes.[49]

The Ornamental—The True

Making use of the title of one of Herbert's prose poems,[50] I am finally introducing the third antinomical pair of categories, which refers mostly to the sphere of aesthetic valuation (although, indirectly, to ethics as well). As in the previous cases, here too one must avoid oversimplification: despite the fact that these two adjectives seem to contain a built-in assessment, the "true" in Herbert's poems is not necessarily placed on a higher level of valuation than the "ornamental." In the early poem "Arion" (SS 82–83, M 31–32), for example, the legendary figure of the ancient dithyramb singer is accompanied by mildly ironic epithets—"the Grecian Caruso," "concertmaster of the ancient world," "cause of giddiness"—but it is also said about him: "the essential thing is that he restores world harmony." Likewise, in the poem "A Tale" (H 30–31, M 44) an ironic presentation of the "poet's" illusions unexpectedly turns into the following conclusion:

> what would the world be
> were it not filled with
> the incessant bustling of the poet
> among the birds and stones

Just as Herbert by no means opts unequivocally for empirical experience against myth, or vice versa, on the level of higher generalizations, there is no unconditional condemnation of "the ornamental" in his poetry on the level of aesthetic categories. The comparison of two poems can be revealing here. In "The Ornament-Makers," a poem that can be read—in a narrower sense—as a stylistic and personal polemic against Konstanty Ildefons Gałczyński and his Stalinist-period popular poetry,[51] the decoration and embellishing of reality are shown to be the domain of hired "stucco-workers" rather than true artists (in the original, *sztukator,* which in fact comes from "stucco," seems to be the ironic echo of the missing word *sztuka,* "art"):

> on the street of festive procession
> the gray prison wall is an eyesore
> an ugly stain on an ideal landscape
>
> the best stucco-workers were called in
> and they painted all night
> even the backs of those on the other side of the wall
>   were painted pink   (H 89)

In specific historical circumstances, then, the role of "the ornamental" can be reduced to obedient whitewash, to hiding the truth under the rosy lies of official optimism—or, in a more sophisticated version, to "the triumphant march of the avant-garde" tolerated, even supported, by the official sponsors in view of its total harmlessness (see "What Mr. Cogito Thinks about Hell," P 74, C 60). An even more complex vision of this problem is presented in an early aesthetic manifesto contained in Herbert's poem "Three Studies on the Subject of Realism" (H 36–38, M 46–47). Here what attempts to be "true" in art is subjected to analysis, and it turns out that "the true," like "the ornamental," comes in many shapes and sizes. Herbert offers a lyrical summary of three tendencies in painting (and the arts in general), which could be called idyllic realism (an idealized and serene reflection of reality), naturalistic realism (an enhancement of reality's dark and depressing sides), and moralistic realism:

> finally they
> the authors of canvases divided into the right side and
>   the left side
> who know only two colours
> colour yes and colour no

It is beyond all understanding why some critics interpret these lines as an ironic unmasking of the practices of Socialist Realism:[52] if the lines remind us of anything, it is rather Herbert's own definition of his poetry as "the moralist's dry poem / yes—yes / no—no" ("A Knocker," H 33, M 45). This sort of art is interested neither in "the ornamental" nor in "the true" as a mirror reflection of reality—its goal is rather to confront the audience with contradictory values and to help them make a worthy choice:

> on to the empty stage
> under a blinding light
> we throw you
> with a shout: choose while there's time
> choose what you're waiting for
> choose

> And to help you we imperceptibly give a nudge to the
> balance

The World of Literary Characters

The values that in Herbert's imagery are associated with symbolic representations of whiteness, light, and air and in his system of ethical and aesthetic categories are identified with abstractness, perfection, and ornamentality, are usually personified in the world of his literary characters by ancient Olympians or inhabitants of the Christian heaven, that is to say, gods or angels.[53] The question of the Greco-Roman or Judeo-Christian provenance of this set of symbols is, as I have noted, relatively irrelevant to Herbert's poetry. More essential is that both gods and angels symbolize the opposite extreme of earth and man with all their grayness, concreteness, imperfection, and truth. I have already quoted the prose poem "Anything Rather Than an Angel," in which the antinomy is very clear-cut. Let me cite a few other examples of Herbert's poems with angels as the chief characters or with Paradise as the background. In the early poem "See" (SS 43, C 5), the tone is set by characteristic epithets: angels are presented as "haughty and very unearthly." Another poem, "The Paradise of the Theologians" (H 122, M 65), presents a deliberately conventional image of Eden; this could be called a pseudo-Classicist Paradise, one much more perfected, trimmed, spruced up, and symmetrical than Paradise in the Bible or folk apocrypha:[54]

> Alleys, long alleys bordered by trees which are as
> carefully trimmed as in an English park. Sometimes an
> angel passes here. His hair is carefully curled, his
> wings rustle with Latin. He holds in his hands a neat
> instrument called a syllogism. He walks quickly with-

out stirring the air or sand. He passes in silence by the
stony symbols of virtues, the pure qualities, the ideas
of objects and many other completely unimaginable
things. He never disappears from sight because here
there are no perspectives. Orchestras and choirs keep
silent yet music is present. The place is empty. The
theologians talk spaciously. This also is supposed to be
a proof.

Peculiar things begin to happen, though, whenever the world of
angels comes in contact with the human world. In the prose poem
"Seven Angels" (H 128) we see a radical reversal of the angel's traditional function as God's messenger bringing the souls of the dead
to the Lord for judgment.[55] The human character in this poem is
very much alive; he is visited each morning by seven angels who
take his heart out of his breast and drink his blood:

Then their wings wither, and their silver faces turn
red. They depart, their sabots thumping heavily. They
leave my heart on a chair like a little empty pot. It
takes all day to refill it, so that the angels won't depart
silvery and winged the next morning.

The abstract perfection, personified by an angel, thus derives the
ability to exist—almost as a vampire does—from the "blood" of
the human, carnal concrete. Once again the only solution is "to
mix a grain of the absolute with a grain of clay." The poem "Report
from Paradise," the source of this quotation, brilliantly transfers
this paradox onto the supra-individual plane. Since even in Paradise
"they were not able to separate exactly the soul from the flesh," the
utopia of the absolute, marred by the inevitable humanity of those
ex-earthling angels, has degraded into a social utopia, a sort of
fairy-tale Socialism:

In paradise the work week is fixed at thirty hours
salaries are higher prices steadily go down

. . . . .

some day God will be seen by all
when it will happen nobody knows

As it is now every Saturday at noon
sirens sweetly bellow

and from the factories go the heavenly proletarians
awkwardly under their arms they carry their wings
   like violins (N 25, M 131)

When faced with the concreteness of the human world, not only
angels but their negative counterparts—devils—lose their perfection and degenerate. I have already quoted "The Homegrown
Devil"; the same idea is exemplified in a short prose poem "A
Devil" (SP 77, M 118), in which the central character is "an utter
failure as a devil." Though the poem contains no direct mention of
his having had contact with humans, one can nonetheless assume
that this devil has been contaminated by human consciousness,
which is marked by doubt and uncertainty; he is distinguished by
the fact that his horns "don't grow outward like other devils' but
inward, into the brains. That's why he suffers so often from
headaches."

Let us return for a moment to the figures of angels. They too
have no shortage of "utter failures," angels contaminated with human imperfection. Perhaps the best known of Herbert's poems on
this subject is "The Seventh Angel" (H 61–63, M 51–52). Its title
character, with the none too angelic name of Shemkel, differs from
his six colleagues by being "black and nervous" and having been
"fined many times / for illegal import of sinners":

> Shemkel Shemkel
> —the angels complain
> why are you not perfect
>
> the Byzantine artists
> when they paint all seven
> reproduce Shemkel
> just like the rest
>
> because they suppose
> they might lapse into heresy
> if they were to portray him
> just as he is
> black nervous
> in his old threadbare nimbus

An even further "humanization"—but this time a forced one—
spoils the angelic perfection of the hero of another well-known
poem, "Preliminary Investigation of an Angel" (N 23–24, M 129–
130).[56] The angel's pure "innocence" (significantly, he is "all / com-

posed of light") becomes tainted with human "blood" again: in this case, however, it is the blood of torture and suffering. Transplanted from the sanctuary of myth into human, historical reality, the angel is tortured, like any man, by nameless interrogators, and his suffering places him, as it does people, "between cloud and mudpuddle." The conclusion of the poem is deliberately ambiguous:

> they hang him head downwards
>
> from the hair of the angel
> drops of wax run down
> and shape on the floor
> a simple prophecy

This could be interpreted as the angel's final victory; despite all the torture, he does not let his deepest secret be wrung from him.[57] At the same time, however, the startling image introduced in the poem's conclusion comes down to a metaphorical identification of the angel with a candle turned upside down: thus, the "light" the angel is "all composed of" turns out to be the mortal light of a candle. And an upside-down candle must either melt away or die out—therein lies the "simplicity" of the prophecy in the wax.

As a matter of fact, "haughty and very unearthly" angels do not appear in Herbert's poetry as frequently as do angelic go-betweens, angels who symbolize a kind of osmosis between heaven and earth. Shemkel and the interrogated angel are heroes whose perfection is marred by their physicality, pain, error, their falling short of the ideal. This is an important point, since it allows us to understand, by way of analogy, the peculiar role played by the god Hermes in Herbert's poetry. In the parallel sphere of pagan mythology, Hermes, like most of the Christian angels, acts as a go-between or intermediary between the world of gods and that of humans. From this point of view, a significant example of Hermes' function is to be found in the prose poem "Attempt to Dissolve Mythology" (N 40, C17), where we witness an operation analogous to that in "Preliminary Investigation of an Angel": the characters are transferred from myth to the historical, human, concrete world. Here, the ancient gods are likened to a clandestine guerrilla unit[58] in a country where a new order has triumphed; gathered "in a shack at the outskirts of town," they come to the conclusion that they "must dissolve the organization, enough senseless conspiracy, [they] must enter this rational society and somehow survive." That it is precisely Hermes who, as the only god, does not yield to the will of the majority, is a significant paradox: he "abstains from voting" and commits suicide by jumping into the river ("They watched him drown, but no one tried to save him"). Faithfulness to the principles comes, as it were, easier to those who know the price of human uncertainty.

At the other extreme in the world of gods, Apollo can be seen as a representative of the purely divine element. Apollo appears in Herbert's poetry with significant frequency, and his portrait can be composed from several separate poems.[59] In the early poem "To Apollo" (SS 21–23),[60] already quoted, the god is shown solely as a statue—he is silent, "with eyes white as a stream," "stone / from his sandals to the ribbon in his hair." Although once, long ago, even in marble form, he was able to incite the speaker's "admiration," now—after the disaster of war—he only appears in his dreams "with the face / of a Persian killed in battle." History's cataclysms have given the lie to the ideals of clarity and harmony as embodied in Apollo:

> the prophecies of poetry are mistaken
> Everything was different
>
> Fire in a poem was one thing
> Fire in a city was another
>
> The heroes did not come back from their expedition
> There were no heroes
> The unworthy survived
>
> I seek the statue
> drowned in my youth
>
> There is only an empty pedestal left—
> a trace of a hand groping for a shape

In the prose poem, or rather parable, entitled "On the Road to Delphi" (H 142, C 14), Apollo appears in a completely different capacity and situation:

> It was on the road to Delphi. I had just passed a red
> rock when from the opposite side Apollo appeared. He
> walked rapidly, without paying attention to anything.
> As he approached I noticed that he was playing with
> the Medusa's head, shriveled and dried from age. He
> was whispering something under his breath. If I heard

correctly, he was repeating: "A craftsman must probe
to the very bottom of cruelty."

This time, the figure of Apollo, the god of the arts and the sun,
is associated not so much with harmony as with inhuman cruelty;
we can assume that his utterance is what he just ordered the Delphic
oracle to tell the pilgrims who would come to it seeking the truth
(Apollo, the official patron of Delphi, arrives from the opposite
direction than the narrator who is on the way there). The head of
Medusa which Apollo is "playing with" (in fact, it was Perseus who
actually killed Medusa) may symbolize the world's ugliness and
horror, which leave Apollo (and Apollonian artists, or "craftsmen,"
as well) morally indifferent, as to toys or games. The same idea—
the inseparability of perfection and indifferent cruelty—is expressed with even greater precision in another of Herbert's "Apollonian" poems, the famous "Apollo and Marsyas" (SP 17–19, M
82–83). This poem has been analyzed so thoroughly by numerous
critics[61] that there is no need for a detailed dissection here. One
point, however, should be emphasized: the poem's basic concept
lies in its attempt to complete the uncompleted story, to finish what
was rarely mentioned in the traditional version of the myth. "The
real duel" between Apollo and Marsyas takes place when the win-
ner of the musical contest, the god, begins to exact payment of his
prize: he starts stripping his opponent—a silenus, and therefore
closer to the humans than to the gods—of his skin. Characterized
with significantly anachronistic epithets such as "the god with
nerves of artificial fibre," Apollo proves to be almost completely (if
we do not count his "shudder of disgust") impervious to Marsyas'
howl; he is perfectly able to calmly "clean his instrument" (did he
perhaps use his lyre's strings as instruments of torture?) and coldly
wonder

> whether out of Marsyas' howling
> there will not some day arise
> a new kind
> of art—let us say—concrete

Even the world of nature ultimately proves to be more sensitive
than the god:

> suddenly
> at his feet
> falls a petrified nightingale

> he looks back
> and sees
> that the hair of the tree to which Marsyas was fastened
>
> is white
>
> completely

All things considered, it might seem that Apollo, the purest representative of the "divine" world, is characterized in Herbert's poetry as an unequivocal symbol of perfection, at once harmonious and haughtily cruel. However, on the very next page after "Apollo and Marsyas" in the volume *Studium przedmiotu*—most likely not a random placement—is the poem "Fragment" (SP 20, M 84), whose final apostrophe associates the same god with entirely opposite values:

> not for the stone wreath of Troy do we implore you o
> Master
> not for a plume of fame white women and gold
> but restore if you can to blemished faces goodness
> and put simplicity into our hands just as you once put
> iron
>
> send down white clouds Apollo white clouds white
> clouds

Even when we allow for an element of uncertainty (the significant "if you can") and even when we assume that the apostrophe is delivered by a speaker who is not identical with the author (most probably, he is a warrior from the *Iliad*), we will still have to agree that in the light of "Fragment" the meaning of the opposition between gods and humans proves to be ambiguous.[62] Man, burdened with all the limitations of his condition, may find a paradoxical consolation in derogating the gods' dignity and deriding their privileges:

> why should the gods be envied?
>
> —for celestial drafts
> —for a botched administration
> —for unsatiated lust
>
> —for a tremendous yawn
> ("Mr. Cogito and Longevity," R 30, CR 25)

He may also desperately reject all forms of mediation between heaven and earth, including the Redemption:

> he shouldn't have sent his son
> he would have been better off reigning
> in the Baroque palace of marble clouds
> on the throne of fear
> with the sceptre of death
> ("Mr. Cogito's Meditation on Redemption," P 67)

Such extreme reactions, however, always coexist with man's need for grace, the latter being a form of mediation between heaven and the human world just as an opposite form of such mediation can be seen in man's efforts to transgress the limits of his condition (symbolized in a couple of Herbert's poems by the flight of Daedalus and modern space flight). Even though man remains chained to the earth, and divine (God's or gods') intervention remains an illusion, Herbert seems to say that what matters is God's and man's striving toward each other.

HERBERT's confrontation of the realms of heritage and disinheritance,—of a symbolic Arcadia or Paradise Lost and expatriation or banishment from it—acquires particular significance in certain poems, where it functions on several different levels at once—the life of an individual, the history of a given nation or civilization, the history of humanity in general. The common denominator here is the notion of *growing up*—growing up from childhood to maturity, from idyllic primordiality to complex modernity, from myth to the knowledge that results from collective experience.

What is most characteristic of Herbert, however, is his ambivalence about assigning values to these extremes. Perhaps the easiest way to shed some light on this problem is to refer to the well-known controversy between Freud and Jung. The three phases in the development of mankind's consciousness as distinguished by J. G. Frazer—the mythological, the religious, and the scientific—Freud compared to the three phases in an individual's growing up, that is, to infancy, childhood, and maturity (and also to the corresponding three phases of the libido, from narcissism to the final turn toward external reality). Having accepted such a model, Freud thus came to the conclusion—one in accord with his overall philosophy, which owed a great deal to the ideology of the Enlightenment—that mythical thinking is a childlike, or even infantile, form of human consciousness, characterized by narcissism and immaturity. Jung, in turn, radically reversed this diagnosis. In his view, mythical thinking had been a phase of maturity and fullness from which mankind had regressed into a secondary infantilism of "scientific" rationalism.[63]

While not referring overtly to this controversy, Herbert nonetheless takes a position toward it as a poet. The implied reasoning in his poetry leads to the conclusion that even though the "heritage" of myth is a phase of "childhood" to which there is no return, it is by no means a stage that can be dismissed or rejected. Let me give one concise example, the prose poem "The Country" (H 115):

> In the very corner of that old map there is the country I long for. It is the homeland of apples, hills, lazy rivers, tart wine, and love. Unfortunately, a great spider has spun its web over that country and closed the dream's toll-gates with gluey saliva.
> It's always like this: an angel with a fiery sword, a spider, a conscience.

The complex meaning of this poem can easily escape the reader's attention; it might seem to carry only a symbolic message, whereas in fact the literal meanings are equally important.[64] "The country" represents both a symbolic Arcadia or Paradise Lost and the geographically and historically specific part of prewar Poland where the poet was born and spent his childhood, inaccessible now because of the postwar shift of the Polish-Soviet border. The poem's figurative language, however, does not serve only to veil meanings which otherwise might fall victim to censorship. The "spider" is not only a transparent pseudonym for the Soviet Union. Let us consider the final sentence, in which "an angel with a fiery sword," "a spider" and "a conscience" are put on the same semantic level, thus identifying mankind's perspective with those of the nation and of the individual. This is a statement of extraordinary significance for the whole of Herbert's poetry. "It's always like this": just as we (the human race) have been banished from Paradise, and just as we are sometimes banished (as a nation or civilization) from our geographical or cultural heritage, so are we also banished from the "dream" of childhood by our mature "conscience," our restless and tormented consciousness. And this is an irreversible process—all our "metamorphoses downward to the sources of history / the lost paradise of childhood in a drop of water" are merely our "shameful dreams" (compare the poem "Shameful Dreams," R 33, CR 28).

In fact, as we shall see in the next chapter, Herbert often seems to contradict his own premises by assuming the "naive" point of view of a child. But these exceptions only confirm the rule, since that way of viewing reality is always subjected to self-irony. In Herbert's poetry there is no returning to childhood, the unconscious, or Paradise Lost: "Herbert's Arcadia has been destroyed by an angel with a fiery sword."[65] A simple—narcissistic, as Freud would have it—"sense of identity" with the world (see poems such as "Sense of Identity" or "Sister," P 11, C 36) is imaginable only, so to speak, in the past tense—in the past tense of childhood, the mists of primordial civilization, mankind's mythical beginnings. The adulthood of both an individual and a civilization is synonymous with the triumph of *principium individuationis*—with a sense of alienation and distance, which condemn man to the human condition and solitary fate and enclose him "in the limits of his own skin" (P 11, C 36). The "dream," however, remains a dream; the "heritage" remains a heritage for whose retrieval one should struggle even though the adult awareness of "disinheritance" be disheartening. In Herbert's poetry man is in precarious balance between these two necessities, two opposed ways of being.

TWO

Metaphors

ZBIGNIEW HERBERT'S poetic world, as I have shown, exists between two opposite poles. These two extremes, which can be called "heritage" and "disinheritance," generate a peculiar tension, highly characteristic of Herbert's poetry. In the next two chapters I will try to explore and explain the nature of that tension. First, however, let me put the conclusions drawn thus far into some order. I have observed that the opposition of heritage and disinheritance, which governs Herbert's imagery and system of values, appears in complementary versions on various structural levels of his poetry, from symbolic key words up to general ethical and aesthetic categories and types of literary characters—as summarized in the following list:

	Heritage	*Disinheritance*
Key words	white, light, air	gray, shadow, earth
Spatial and temporal categories	the Mediterranean tradition	the contemporary world of the East European
Cognitive and ontological categories	the mythical reality approachable through culture	the empirical reality approachable through the senses
Ethical and aesthetic categories	the abstract, the perfect, the ornamental	the tangible, the erroneous, the true
Literary characters	gods or angels	people

The most important thing about this classification is that its two opposite ends are in a dynamic equilibrium. The mechanism of constant confrontation in Herbert's poetry by no means leads toward the absolute prevalence of one of the opposed sets of values. Once in a while one set can gain predominance, but only temporarily, only within a single poem. To return to a highly characteristic example I have already cited, the poem "Apollo and Marsyas," even with all its ambiguity taken into account, is undoubtedly a defense of what is "true," imperfect, tangible, and human, against what is "ornamental," perfect, abstract, and divine; it is a defense of Marsyas' suffering against Apollo's indifference. Yet the very next poem in the collection *Studium przedmiotu*, "Fragment," appears as an apostrophe to Apollo himself, ending with a highly significant request: "send down white clouds Apollo white clouds white clouds," where the cluster of symbolic white, airy, and divine elements is obviously viewed as a positive and desired value.

It is precisely this suspension *between* heritage and disinheritance that characterizes the position of the implied author in Herbert's poetry. The implied author is portrayed as a man exiled from Paradise and dispossessed of traditional values—but, at the same time, a man who is painfully conscious of what he has lost and who never accepts his loss. Accordingly, what can be considered the basic structural pattern in Herbert's poetry is not only the incessant confrontation, which I have explored thus far, but also the *mutual unmasking* of the two sets of antinomical values and two types of reality: the reality of heritage and the reality of disinheritance.

This mutual unmasking can be carried out in two distinctly different ways. In the attempt to discern and describe these two methods of Herbert, it will be useful to refer to the well-known distinction between two figures of speech: metaphor and irony.[1] What they share is an indirect approach to speaking about reality: each of them consists of a plane of meaning that is "represented" and one that is "not represented." In the case of metaphor, there is no essential contradiction between these two semantic levels; "what is said" and "what is meant" are placed in a relationship of mutual resemblance. Irony is an entirely different matter. The simplest definition of irony (considered as a form of speech) states that it is a way of speaking in which "one meaning is stated and a different, usually antithetical, meaning is intended."[2] "What is said" and "what is meant" are related by their opposition or contradiction.

For years it has been a critical commonplace to distinguish irony as the most conspicuous feature of Herbert's poetic method. It is certainly true that irony is highly significant in his poetry and is brought by him to heights of artistic perfection. In most cases, though, by "irony" the critics tend to mean something very vague and general, much in the spirit of Cleanth Brooks's well-known definition of irony as a universal mechanism of poetry as such.[3] Such an approach results in virtually nothing being said about the specific character of this particular poetry. Therefore, the notion of irony must be defined—I will try to do this in Chapter 3—with the utmost precision, and its use and functioning must be examined closely. In order to do this, however, I must first distinguish between Herbert's ironies and metaphors and pay close attention to the specific qualities of the latter. For it is also the use of metaphor that reveals the individual nature of Herbert's poetry and its unique vision of the world.

Like irony, which will later be seen both as a figure of speech and as a more general attitude, I refer to metaphor here both in its narrow sense of a stylistic device and as a "great metaphor" subordinating the meanings of an entire text. I should repeat at this point that the stylistic level of Herbert's work has been strangely neglected by the critics.[4] With the exception of some marginal remarks by certain critics,[5] almost no one has dealt seriously and in detail with Herbert's poetic use of language.[6] On the contrary, there exists a persistent myth about the perfect stylistic "transparency" of his poetry and its supposed affinity with the poetics of Tadeusz Różewicz.[7] To a certain extent the poet himself is to blame for these misunderstandings; in interviews and essays he has declared himself more than once on the side of language that would not be an end in itself but would strive for an ideal of "semantic transparency."[8] "I would wish my poems to consist of transparent words and transparent arrangements of words," he said in a fictitious dialogue included as an introduction in his *Poezje wybrane* [Selected Poems]; "That is to say, I would not wish my words to focus the reader's attention and to make him exclaim 'Oh, what a master he is,' but instead to show reality in as clear and transparent a way as possible." Later in that same statement Herbert's wish appears to have specific historical and ethical motivations:

> Language is an impure tool of expression. It is tortured, banalized, subjected to shabby tricks every day. Therefore, the poets' dream is to reach to the words'

pristine sense, to give the proper word to things, as
Norwid says. "Let words mean only what they mean,
and not whom they were used against." This is another
quotation, from another great poet.[9]

Here an essential point is made more precise. The defense of the
transparency of language is in fact a defense of language against
deformations resulting from sociotechnical manipulation—but
Herbert does not reject the sort of "opacity" that results from poetic organization of language. His "search for an adequate word"[10]
does not exclude a word transformed or arranged in a poetic way.[11]
Contrary to Tadeusz Różewicz, who, in accordance with his
openly expressed doubts as to culture's possibilities, has also rejected metaphor as a supposedly hollow ornament, Herbert is far
from such easy extremism. It is a fact that in one of his poems he
says about his lyrical *porte-parole:*

> He would rarely soar
> on the wings of a metaphor
> and then he fell like Icarus
> into the embrace of the Great Mother
> ("Mr. Cogito and the Imagination," R 22, CR 17)

But it is also significant that the dislike of metaphor is presented by
the means of a metaphor. Suspended like Icarus between the sky of
myth and the earth of empirical experience, Herbert in his use of
language is also constantly balancing between poetic organization
and semantic transparency, between the conventional idiom of poetry and colloquial spontaneity.[12] It is exactly this dynamic and
complex equilibrium of contrasts and tensions between styles that
will prove essential for the functioning of the mechanisms of irony
(which I shall examine later). For the time being, it is sufficient to
be aware that Herbert, contrary to superficial appearances and to
his own declarations, by no means rejects poetic methods for organizing language.

AMONG those poetic methods for organizing language, Herbert's
use of metaphor plays a special role: both metaphor considered as
a single figure of speech and metaphor that provides a semantic
axis for a whole poem. Both Herbert's "great" and "small" metaphors are marked by their characteristic *paradoxicality.*[13] The essence
of metaphor consists, by definition, in stating a similarity between

two objects. But, if Herbert states any similarity, he does so only, as it were, to place the essential contradiction of the two compared objects against the background of their apparent analogy and thus to make the contradiction stand out as clearly as possible.

In other words, Herbert, like anyone who uses metaphors, uses them to state indirectly that object A is "in fact" object B.[14] What is characteristic of his individual method is that we are supposed to be surprised not so much by the mere semantic distance between A and B, and not even so much by their belonging to two opposed and contrasted worlds, as by the fact that these are two particular worlds: the world of myth (in many specific senses of this word) and the world of experience. A metaphor of this kind could be termed an *unmasking metaphor.* Its hidden meaning comes down to the statement that "from the point of view of myth, A seems to be A, but experience teaches us that A is in fact B," or the other way around, "according to experience, A seems to be A, but myth lets us realize that A is in fact B." The mutual unmasking of "heritage" from the viewpoint of "disinheritance" and vice versa, thus even takes place at the level of the elementary stylistic molecules.

Let me cite some examples, confining them at first to figures of speech that could be considered classic metaphors in the narrow sense of the word:

> Over the megaphones was sung
> an anachronistic ballad
> about Poles and bayonets
>
> *A tenor struck like a riding-whip*
> and after every verse
> a list was published of live torpedoes
>   ("Farewell to September," SS 7, M 30)
>
> On the plain that town flat like an iron sheet
>
> . . . . .
>
> there are troops *a big rattle of barracks* on the outskirts
>   ("Naked Town," SP 46, M 100)

These two metaphors cannot be interpreted in any other way than as clear examples of the unmasking of the world of myth by the world of experience. In both cases we find the characteristic implied statement of a metaphor: "A seems to be A, whereas in fact A is B." A tenor seems to sing with a clear voice a patriotic song, whereas in fact his voice strikes like a riding-whip; military barracks seem to be the place for real men and their serious affairs, whereas in fact they are an enormous toy rattle.[15] What is particularly characteristic of Herbert is that connotations of the words "riding-whip" and "toy rattle" carry meanings that are exactly contradictory to those brought by the connotations surrounding the words "[patriotic] ballad" and "[military] barracks." The very metaphoric juxtaposition contradicts certain established myths and compromises them. Herbert seems to say: according to the universally accepted myth, a song rousing people to fight expresses the will of the nation—but according to our experience, such a song can be nothing more than a riding-whip (an instrument that, significantly, is anachronistic, aristocratic, and brutal at the same time), by which the nation is driven on like a balky saddle horse. According to another popular myth, the army is a means for defending important values against outside menaces—our experience, however, again teaches us that under certain circumstances the army can be merely a toy, for example in the hands of dictators.

What takes place in metaphors of this kind, then, is the unmasking of mythologized notions by concrete, empirical experience. But such unmasking can take the reverse direction as well:

> Nike is most beautiful at the moment
> when she hesitates
> her right hand beautiful as a command
> *rests against the air*   ("Nike Who Hesitates," SS 74, M 27)

> *Gothic towers of needles* in the valley of a stream
> not far from Mount Tamalpais   ("Sequoia," P 38, C 45)

Here it is the mythical context that contradicts the common experience. Experience would suggest that it is impossible for someone's hand to "rest against the air" and that sequoias are just tall conifers; "in fact," however, within the sphere of myth and art Nike—both as a goddess and as a sculpture—is able to perform that impossible act,[16] and sequoias (considered, as explained in more detail in the rest of the poem, as witnesses to the history of human civilization) can be equated in function to Gothic cathedrals. While in the previous examples the common, down-to-earth experience provided a point of reference in unmasking one or another (nationalistic, jingoistic, and so on) myth, Herbert's poetry offers the opposite option as well: as in the latter examples, the reality of myth can serve as a point of reference in unmasking what seems to be the truth provided by sensual data or commonsense logic.

It is striking that in both cases the final effect is a metaphoric juxtaposition that is actually close to a paradox: the semantic contradiction between the two components of the metaphor is more "visible" than their mutual similarity. As a matter of fact, if we look closer at Herbert's figures of speech, we cannot overlook his tendency toward oxymoronic juxtaposition or paradoxical statements. Here is a handful of examples of typical oxymorons:

> I the exile of obvious forms
> preach your *motionless dance*   ("Architecture," SS 40)

> and perhaps we both
> who are made of blood and illusion
> will finally free ourselves
> from the *oppressive levity* of appearance
>   ("A Parable of King Midas," SS 71, M 26)

> when in the other mountains
> I drink *dry water*   ("*** What will happen . . . ," N 53, M 126)

> in town *an epidemic broke out*
> *of the instinct of self-preservation*
>   ("Mr. Cogito on Upright Attitudes," P 75, C 64)

> he would like to remain faithful
> to *uncertain clarity*
>   ("Mr. Cogito and the Imagination," R 24, CR 19)

This list could be complemented by numerous examples of equally exposed paradoxes, such as the sentences "Let us not let the dead die" ("Three Poems from Memory," SS 10) and "They left their traces on a wave . . . they have their shelter in the bell of air" ("A Ballad on Us Not Dying," SS 61). These oxymorons and paradoxes are quite abundant for someone who is popularly labeled a Classicist. Be that as it may, their presence is a clear sign of the constant functioning of Herbert's antithetic imagery, which leaves its mark even on the stylistic level of his poetry. Not only his oxymorons and paradoxes but also his other figures of speech and rhetorical devices, as a rule, contain an antithetic core, that is, they are based on a mutual confrontation and unmasking of contradictory meanings, whose opposition is made even more conspicuous by their apparent similarity or closeness. A figure Herbert often uses, for example, is the device that would have been defined in Classical rhetoric as a syllepsis—the subordination of two syntactic elements to one superior element, which, while being grammatically and syntactically correct, emphasizes their mutual logical and semantic incompatibility:

> instead of *cultivating*
> *pansies and onomatopeias*
> he plants thorny exclamations
> invectives and treatises
> ("Mr. Cogito and the Poet of Certain Age," P 42)

Finally, a particularly telling evidence of Herbert's active attitude toward language and, at the same time, of his antithetic imagery is provided by his numerous transformations of set phrases. As with metaphor in the narrow sense, such operations contribute, as a rule, to the mutual unmasking of two opposed worlds—if a hackneyed expression contains the quintessence of either a myth or a common experience, its transformation is a particularly effective means of contradicting such a view, since the transformation throws the reader off his mental balance. In the poem "Farewell to September," we read:

> The commander . . .
> chanted: not one button

> The buttons mocked:
> We shan't give we shan't give the boys
> sewn flatly on to the heath   (SS 7, M 30)

The legendary slogan devised by military commander Rydz-Śmigły in 1939, "We shall give [the Germans] not one button," is here subjected to a paradoxical reversal: the concrete experience of soldiers "sewn flatly on to the heath," lying flat under fire with the buttons of their uniforms pressed down into the earth, is a contradiction of the boastful myth created by the marshal. A similar meaning is implied in the phrase *Chłopcy malowani wapnem* (Boys painted with lime) from the prose poem "War" (H 131), which is a paradoxical elaboration of a hackneyed expression *chłopcy malowani* (painted, that is, handsome, colorful, boys) from a popular military song. Sometimes, however, the transformation of a set phrase works in the opposite direction. The poem "Mr. Cogito and the Movement of Thoughts" (P 24, C 41) opens with statements indicating that it is rather the commonsense notions contained in a "popular expression" that the poem will negate by taking the expression literally:

> Thoughts cross the mind
> says the popular expression
>
> the popular expression
> overestimates the movement of thoughts
>
> most of them
> stand motionless
> in the middle of a dull landscape
> of ashy hills
> parched trees

It is indeed strange to what degree Herbert's frequent linguistic puns and transformations escape the critics' attention. Some of his poems are just variations on certain set phrases (for instance, those in the titles "Salt of the Earth," SS 80, and "The Church Mouse," SP 72, the latter being a part of the proverbial comparison "poor as a church mouse"); in others we encounter occasional puns, sometimes playing on the antithetical meanings of words. And yet the sanctified critical opinion maintains that in contemporary Polish poetry Herbert occupies a position diametrically opposed to that of the so-called linguistic school. It is true that for Herbert language is not the primary concern—but this does not mean that language appears to him as a completely transparent, imperceptible windowpane between the object and the perceiving subject.

HERBERT's antithetic logic and imagery, and the means of unmasking he uses, reveal their presence even more clearly in the higher structural level of his poetry, where they provide the basis for the most characteristic of his "great metaphors" and in that capacity function as the foundation of many of his poems. This metaphoric skeleton is particularly visible in Herbert's brief prose poems. Let us notice how persistently the same syntactic pattern recurs in many of them—the pattern that in each case can be reduced to the model we have already encountered: "It seems that A is A, whereas in fact A is B." Sometimes this is presented in a literal, bare version:

> *In appearance* a drop of rain on a beloved face . . . *In*
> *fact* the period . . . is a bone protruding from the sand,
> a snapping shut, a sign of a catastrophe.
> ("Period," N 44, M 136)

> The peaceful face of a miller *to all appearances* . . .
> *But if you look within it:* a nest of worms, the interior of
> an ant-hill.   ("The Clock," SP 75)

At other times, the same logical mechanism is not so clearly
visible or is subjected to syntactic transformations. Nevertheless,
the presence of expressions such as "really," "in fact," "true," and
so on serves each time to indicate that the poem is still based on the
same model of appearance-rectified-by-truth:

> In a small hut at the edge of a forest lived a mother
> and her little son . . . But the mother died. The son
> was left. *In fact,* it was a fairly old bed-side rug.
> ("Mother and Her Little Son," H 110)

> The *true* history of the prince Minotaur is told in the
> script Linear A, which has not yet been deciphered.
> Notwithstanding later gossip he was the authentic son
> of King Minos and Pasiphaë.
> ("History of the Minotaur," P 51, C 47)

It can also happen that the "true" version is presented without
qualification, whereas the appropriate expressions indicate instead
that an "appearance" or "false version" has been rejected:

> *I can't understand how it is possible* to write poems
> about the moon. The moon is fat and slovenly. It picks
> the noses of chimneys. Its favorite occupation is to
> crawl underneath beds and smell shoes.
> ("The Moon," H 172)

> *I had always suspected* that this city is a fake. But only
> during a hazy noon in early spring, when the air smells
> of starch, did I discover what *the hoax* consisted of. We
> live inside a closet . . .   ("In a Closet," H 164)

> *They say* he became deaf—*but it isn't true*

the demons of his hearing worked tirelessly
and the dead lake never slept in the shells of his ears
("Beethoven," R 54, CR 49)

the famous shout on Mount Taches
is mistakenly interpreted by sentimental poets
they [Cyrus' warriors] simply found the sea that is the
    exit from the dungeon   ("Anabasis," R 50, CR 45)

Another variant appears in the poems in which the pattern "It
seems that . . . whereas in fact . . ." has been reversed: Where the
"true" version is presented first and only after its introduction is
the "false" version refuted:

    Violins are naked. They have thin arms. Clumsily
    they try to protect themselves with them. They cry
    from shame and cold. *That's why. And not,* as the music
    critics maintain, so that it will be more beautiful. *This
    is not true.*   ("Violins," H 107, C11)

    As a matter of fact elephants are very sensitive and
    nervous . . . I myself knew an elephant who fell in love
    with a hummingbird. He lost weight, did not sleep,
    and finally died of a heart attack. *Those who do not
    know about the nature of elephants* have been saying: he
    was so slobbish.   ("Elephant," H 155, M 69)

Finally, it is sometimes the case that the constant model of reasoning is completely concealed, that if it reveals itself, it does so
not as a clear-cut syntactic contradiction but in a more discreet way.
In the prose poem "Wringer" (H 167, M 72), for example, the title
contraption appears to be in fact an instrument of torture employed
by "the inquisitors"; the "false" notion, according to which a
wringer is just a wringer, is not expressed directly or commented
upon—it is enough that such a notion naturally exists in the mind
of the reader. In another prose poem, "Hell" (H 126), we encounter
what is to all intents and purposes a description of an ordinary
apartment house, from its roof to a café on its first floor; only the
title suggests that in fact A is B, the apartment house equals Hell.[17]
    One could say, then, that even though not all poems of this kind
are based on a direct use of the logical pattern "It seems that A is
A, whereas in fact A is B," the guiding principle in a great many
of Herbert's poems is unmasking, revealing the *true, genuine* nature

of an object, regardless of whether what is being unmasked is a myth (as in "The Moon," "Violins," "History of the Minotaur," or "Anabasis") or a common experience (as in "The Clock," "Wringer," or "Hell"). The unmasking takes place, paradoxically, even when the speaker states that he has not succeeded in confirming his suspicions, in catching an object in the act of removing its mask:

> Inanimate objects are always correct and cannot, unfortunately, be reproached with anything. I have never observed a chair shift from one foot to another, or a bed rear on its hind legs.   ("Objects," H 113, M 63)

> In front of the mirror in my parents' bedroom lay a pink conch. I used to approach it on tiptoes, and with a sudden movement put it against my ears. I wanted to surprise it one day when it wasn't longing with a monotonous hum for the sea. Although I was small I knew that even if we love someone very much, at times it happens that we forget about it.
> ("Conch," H 114, C 10)

Examples of this kind lead us to the question of the specific meanings and forms of the unmaskings that take place in Herbert's poetry. Unmasking means revealing someone's true face, laying bare the truth of something that was concealed by some false appearance. The above-quoted poems, which speak more or less directly about appearance or falseness on the one hand and reality or truth on the other, exemplify only the most overt form of unmasking: cases in which there is a partial or a complete exposure of the poem's logical skeleton. We can speak of unmasking in other poems as well, in which it takes on a more indirect shape—*a different way of looking* at a given object (which can, in practice, be an inanimate or animate object, an artifact, a well-known event, a mythical, literary, or historic figure, and so on). The phrase "a different way of looking" can be understood quite literally here, as a specific point of view, angle, perspective, or focus that differs from the norm.[18] Following these optical associations, we can distinguish several such ways of looking:

Looking from the Other Side

Under normal circumstances it would be hard to imagine an observer able to see the reverse side of the objects presented in a one-dimensional painting. Yet in "Mona Lisa" Herbert resorts to this apparently impossible way of looking, specifically in order to unmask an object.[19] I have already mentioned that the "abnormal" optics of this poem are realistically motivated. The observer, whose dream of seeing the famous painting—which symbolized for him the heritage of the Mediterranean tradition in its purest form—had been unfulfilled for years, has finally arrived at the Louvre. Having overcome many difficulties, he now views the painting in a state of high emotion: for him it is the moment when his dreams and expectations are confronted by the reality. He fixes his gaze on the portrait so intensely that the flat painting acquires, as it were, a third dimension—Mona Lisa appears as "convex / as if constructed out of lenses / concave landscape for a background." The picture develops optical depth; now it becomes possible to perceive what is located between the first-plane figure and its background:

> between the blackness of her back
> which is like a moon in clouds
>
> and the first tree of the surroundings
> is a great void froths of light

There is something more to it than just optical three-dimensionality: to mention the "blackness" of La Gioconda's back means that the observer *sees* it, so he must have placed himself between the figure and the background. This is confirmed by the refrain-like return of the same motif: in the final part of the poem the speaker identifies the painting's background with his own life, an identification that indicates that his point of view is indeed located, contrary to the laws of optics, behind Mona Lisa's back:

> between the blackness of her back
> and the first tree of my life
>
> lies a sword
> a melted precipice

The element of unmasking in such a way of looking seems more obvious now. If we are to assume that the narrator's own life is also a component of the background—the background against which myth (in this particular case, a legendary artifact) is *normally* situated—then it is only the "abnormal" way of looking from behind, from the usually invisible side, that permits the exposure of the reverse side of the myth and the perception of the myth as isolated and separated from the background of life. La Gioconda appears not only inaccessible but also "hewed off from the meat of life / abducted from home and history."

Looking beneath the Surface

This particular way of seeing things differently—a look beneath the surface of an object, within it, into its interior—is perhaps the most natural and comprehensible in its symbolic function. Here, in full, is the prose poem "The Clock" (SP 75):

> The peaceful face of a miller to all appearances, full
> and shiny as an apple. Only a single dark hair moves
> across it. But if you look within it: a nest of worms,
> the interior of an ant-hill. And this is supposed to lead
> us to eternity.

The great metaphor of this brief poem is founded, obviously, on the opposition of an external appearance with an essence hidden beneath its surface. What primarily makes the metaphor accurate is the fact that the opposition corresponds in an exceptionally fortunate way with the visual contrast between the symmetrical and orderly look of the clock's dial and its complicated and seemingly chaotic works. (Another correspondence is suggested by the reference to the archetypal motif of an apple with a worm hidden in it.) Thus, the logic of the image itself enables the poem to confront and unmask two opposed notions of time and of human existence: "to all appearances" it seems that the flow of time leads us harmoniously towards eternity: "in fact," the nature of time is unpredictable and destructive.[20]

The motif of a "look inside" appears in an interesting, humorous, but also dramatic version in the poem "Silk of a Soul" (H 72, M 56). The narrator here is tormented by his awareness that he knows his lover only as an external appearance, through sensual perception:

> I must
> peek inside her
> to see what she wears
> at her centre

This resolve, which at first could be considered a mere figure of speech for learning the contents of the lover's soul, is subsequently reduced to its literal meaning in an unexpected and grotesque manner:

> when she slept
> with her lips open
> I peeked

The "peek inside" brings disappointment—a disappointment of a different kind from what we might expect, because it results not as much from the contrast between outside and inside, as from the dissonance between the narrator's expectations and the reality:

> I was expecting
> branches
> I was expecting
> a bird
> I was expecting
> a house
> by a lake great and silent
>
> but there
> on a glass counter
> I caught sight of a pair
> of silk stockings

We are already familiar with the example of "Wooden Die," in which what seems to be the ultimate attainment of the essence hidden beneath the surface turns out to be just another illusion: "Even if it is quickly cut in two, immediately its inside becomes a wall and there occurs the lightning-swift transformation of a mystery into a skin."

Looking Back into the Past

The examples I have just analyzed are spatial metaphors: a look from the other side or beneath the surface takes in, as a rule, one or another concrete object (or person, landscape, and so on). In Herbert's work there also exist equally numerous examples of "looking differently" not so much at an object as at an event, a story, or an anecdote; in other words, examples in which the field swept by the glance of the observer is not so much space as time. One possibility is, for instance, a look back into what had happened, a reconstruction of the supposed past of a given object that is at odds with its present form of existence:

> At the table, one should sit with composure and not
> daydream. Let us remember how much effort was
> needed in order for the rough sea currents to assume
> the shape of sedate wood grain. A moment of inatten-
> tion, and everything can flow away.
> ("Be Careful with the Table," SP 80)

> Who ever thought a warm neck would become an
> armrest, or legs eager for flight and joy could stiffen
> into four simple stilts? Armchairs were once noble
> flower-eating creatures. However, they allowed them-
> selves too easily to be domesticated and today they are
> the most wretched species of quadrupeds.
> ("Armchairs," SP 81, M 121)

Like the other methods of "looking differently," this method can
be applied to persons as well as to inanimate objects. Just as a reconstruction of "the past" of a table or armchairs reveals their
"once" having been rough seas or four-footed animals, for example, the poem "Curatia Dionisia" (N 39), a description of a se-
pulchral monument to a Roman courtesan, "looks back into the
past" in the sense that it reconstructs her hypothetical biography.

Looking Forward into the Future

What seems to be even more characteristic of Herbert is a reversed
perspective, that is, a method of looking that focuses on the continuation of a certain traditional anecdote (as preserved in myth or
a mythologized literary work), a continuation that is usually passed
over in silence by the canonical, standard version of the story. Even
though we know, for example, what was the stake in the musical
duel of Apollo and Marsyas, the traditional version of the mythological story ends with the victory of the god and never mentions
what happened after it. Herbert locates the final point differently:

> The *real* duel of Apollo
> with Marsyas
> (absolute ear
> versus immense range)
> takes place in the evening
> when *as we already know*

the judges
have awarded victory to the god

In fact, the whole poem narrates the "sequel" to the mythical story—a continuation that, usually prudishly omitted because of its macabre character,[21] is even more interesting to Herbert as a chance to unmask the "real" import of the myth. "Elegy of Fortinbras," which resumes the dramatic action exactly where Shakespeare stopped it at the end of *Hamlet,* is based, of course, on an analogous principle. And in "Old Prometheus" (P 53) the myth, which usually ends with Prometheus bound to the rock, likewise receives an unexpected sequel—the mythical rebel is shown in his old age, when he has accepted, as it were, the Marxist conception of freedom and does not mind if what he won by his rebellion is used to suppress other rebellions:

> He is writing his memoirs. In them he attempts to explain the position of a hero within a system of necessities, to reconcile the contradictory notions of existence and fate . . .
> The fire crackles in the fireplace. On the wall there is a stuffed eagle and a letter of gratitude from the tyrant of the Caucasus, who, thanks to Prometheus's discovery, could burn down a rebellious city.
> Prometheus laughs softly. Now this is his only way of expressing disagreement with the world.

Poems of this kind—including "Hakeldama" (P 56), in which the high priests of Jerusalem deliberate on "what to do with the silver coins / which Judas has thrown at their feet"—could be defined as unmaskingly apocryphal:[22] what is unveiled here is the element of a story that is usually passed over in silence by the standard version but is a logical assumption or consequence of the events of the myth. The apocryphal approach can also be seen in that the focus is on hypothetical supplements of a myth that, despite all their logical justification, utterly contradict the sanctified image of a hero or event and thus are something of a taboo for the canonical version. As a matter of fact, however, as with every bit of apocrypha, poems of this kind deal with taboos not out of willfulness but from a natural curiosity: What, actually, did stripping Marsyas of his skin look like, and did Apollo witness it? How did Fortinbras do after he seized power in Denmark? What happened to Prometheus after he grew old? What did the high priests do with the thirty pieces of silver?

Looking that Takes in the Background

This leads us to Herbert's next "optical" device, which also has something in common with the apocryphal technique. The canonical version of a myth or a stereotyped image of an object usually isolates the character or object to a certain extent, focusing on the central figure in the plot or on the object's schematic features. It is sometimes enough just to take the background or surrounding context into consideration to perform another unmasking, another discovery that in fact the true image of a given person or thing differs from its appearance. For example, the prose poem "The Sacrifice of Iphigenia" (H 161, C 15), instead of focusing on the figure of Iphigenia at the stake as would the traditional version, first reconstructs the perspectives and thoughts of the surrounding characters—Agamemnon, Hippias, Calchas—and finally places the central figure of the drama (who is mentioned only casually and seen only indirectly, through the eyes of other characters) against an even wider background:

> The chorus placed on the hillside takes in the world
> with its correct proportions. The small shining bush of
> the pyre, white priests, purple kings, loud copper and
> the miniature fires of soldiers' helmets, all this against
> a background of bright sand and the immense colour
> of the sun.
> The view is superb, with the help of the proper
> perspective.

The expressions "with its correct proportions" and "the proper perspective" obviously have an ironic ring to them (we realize that in fact the perspective of the myth with its focus on the figure of Iphigenia is more accepted here than the relativistic perspective of purely visual experience imposed by the whole poem). Nevertheless, the widening of the field of vision does introduce a new way of looking at a traditional motif, and thus allows for a confrontation of myth and experience.[23]

Looking that Focuses upon a Detail

More frequent among Herbert's operations is the introduction of a
reverse perspective: the observer's gaze detects one detail or another
that ordinarily would dissolve in the larger picture and be overlooked; his focusing upon this isolated detail again results in the
unmasking of one "appearance" or another, revealing what is
"true." An almost clinical example of this technique can be found
in the poem "Tamarisk" (SP 62, M 109), where the speaker—we
may already know that it is Homer[24]—rejects his usual perspective,
epic panorama, in favor of a seemingly insignificant detail:

> I was talking of battles
>
> . . . . .
>
> I was talking of the sea tempest
> the crumbling of walls
> wheat burning
> and hills overthrown
> and I forgot about the tamarisk

The bard focuses on this particular detail because of the solidarity
he feels with his heroes, for this is precisely the perspective of a
slain warrior:

> when he lies down
> pierced by a javelin
> and the lips of his wound
> slowly close
> he sees
> neither sea
> nor city
> nor friend
> he sees
> just before his face
> the tamarisk

This identification between an empirical perspective focusing
upon a concrete detail and an attitude of solidarity with the defeated
deserves to be remembered as an important clue that will lead us in
other directions. Meanwhile, let me quote some other examples.
"Rosy Ear," for instance, which I have already cited, is a poem in
which a sudden glimpse of a certain detail of the lover's body—her

ear lit from behind by a lamp[25]—allows the speaker to see a "mystery" in what had seemed to be his empirical knowledge of her ("I thought / but I know her so well / we have been living together so many years"). "The Crypt" (H 124) is yet another example of focusing upon a detail:

> I still can straighten the holy picture, so that your
> reconciliation with necessity can be known, and also
> adjust the sash, so that the inscription "to our dearest"
> be a source of tears. But what to do with the fly, with
> the black fly, which creeps into the half-closed mouth
> and takes from it the remaining crumbs of the soul.

Here the appearances—"reconciliation with necessity" ascribed to the corpse and the affected grief of the mourners—are questioned and unmasked by the sudden interference of a dissonant detail that does not fit into the larger picture and immediately draws the observer's undivided attention. Likewise, in another prose poem, "A Still Life" (H 156), the observer's gaze, gradually concentrating upon a detail (all the more striking because it is an *invisible* detail—a piece of the void), appears as an indirect way of unmasking the *nature morte* as a portrayal of nature deliberately put to death by the art:

> With artful carelessness these shapes forcibly de-
> tached from life have been spilled onto the table: a fish,
> an apple, a handful of vegetables mixed with flowers.
> A dead leaf of light and a small bird with a bloodied
> head have been added. In its petrified claws the bird
> clutches a little planet, made of the void and the air
> that had been taken away.

HAVING CITED A number of Herbert's typical "great metaphors," I cannot avoid certain suspicions—suspicions connected with the fundamental distinction already introduced between metaphor and irony. I have said that, contrary to irony, a speaker who uses a metaphor basically "says what he means." Is this always true? Was it true in all examples quoted?

Any answer has to include a solution to the question of *who* actually is the speaker in a given poem and what is the nature of the distance between the speaker and the implied author. It is enough to consider the examples employed thus far to realize that there are various possibilities at hand. They range from the extreme of, say, "Mona Lisa" (where the speaker is basically identified with the implied author, and the central metaphor of "looking from behind" has to be taken at face value as a confrontation between myth and experience) to the extreme of some of Herbert's brief prose poems, the "nursery tales" or "fables,"[26] which display an obvious distance between the implied author and the speaker he "employs." The latter is a deliberately introduced "naive speaker," who usually represents the viewpoint of a child and attempts to unmask the illusion (embodied either in myth and artistic convention or in empirical and commonsense opinions) by revelations from a childlike (or quasi-childlike) imagination.[27]

The point is that Herbert's implied author cannot fully assent to the truth of *such* a kind of unmasking; he cannot adopt it as his own cognitive perspective. After all, he has been irrevocably expelled from the Paradise of the child's consciousness into an adult's awareness of disinheritance. Therefore, a certain, more or less noticeable distance invariably emerges in such situations. It is particularly obvious when the childlike use of language or logic displays all its comical awkwardness:

> Bears can be divided into brown ones and white
> ones and also into paws, heads, and bodies. They have
> kind muzzles, and tiny eyes. They love to eat a lot,
> those bears. ("Bears," H 136)

> The path runs barefoot into the forest. In the forest
> are many trees, a cuckoo, Hansel and Gretel, and other
> little animals. ("The Forest," H 152)

In other words, these are the situations in which the childlike narrator *unmasks himself,* or rather: unmasks his own naiveté. In some of the poems of this sort, the distance borders on the specific kind of irony that is called *"ingénu* irony" by the theoreticians.[28] The center of gravity can, however, shift: in "The Clock," for instance, the central metaphor that compares the clock's works to a nest of worms can be both taken seriously by the reader (as a visual analogy and as a philosophical statement on the nature of time) and dismissed by him (as the childish fears of the speaker, placed by the implied author in ironic parentheses).[29] There are also poems in which the "naive" point of view undergoes a dynamic change: the childish narrator "grows up" in the course of his monologue, finally assuming a mature consciousness.[30] Be that as it may, we must be aware that the borderline between Herbert's metaphors and ironies is somewhat blurred. In fact, there is an intermediate zone between them, where it is difficult to assess whether the unmasking is carried out by means of a direct confrontation between the external appearance and the inner truth, or by a much more complex, indirect and ambiguous method—the method of irony.

THREE

Ironies

IF IRONY serves the same principle, that of unmasking, as metaphor does, the former is undoubtedly a more difficult and subtle method. Despite that difficulty—or perhaps because of it—Herbert resorts to it much more often. One could even say he makes irony his chief and programmatic poetic method. It is impossible to overlook this fact: there are several poems in which the word "irony" is used overtly as synonymous with the attitude the implied author considers more or less his own (more or less, because sometimes irony itself is viewed from an ironic distance).

Let us review some of the essential contexts in which the word "irony" appears in Herbert's poetry. One of his early poems, "The Altar" (SS 65), consists of a description of an ancient bas-relief:

> A sandal and a piece of foot they have been guarded by
>   the goddess of Irony
> as have the robes' folds from which you will easily
>   read
> the gesture of beautifully raised arms and this is indeed
>   all
> there were no hands playing the horns of sacrificial
>   animals
>
> You do not know what word of yours and what shape
>   perhaps a flimsy one
> will be preserved by a wrinkle of stone—not what you
>   think is yourself—
> and you do not know whether your blood and bones
>   or perhaps your eyelash
> will be chosen and laid in the kind earth where statues
>   mellow

In this early poem, the very notion of irony is already marked by a certain paradoxicality. "The goddess of Irony" preserves the past and saves it from ruin; however, she saves—and therein the irony—only some accidental fragments of the past, fragments from which one has to laboriously reconstruct the whole. Irony, then, is seen here as an objectively existing chance element in history and human memory, independent of anyone's conscious intent.

Another personification of irony, offered by the prose poem "Mad Woman" (H 121, C 9), appears in an unexpectedly different context:

> Her burning look holds me tightly in an embrace.
> She says words mixed with dreams. She invites. You
> will be happy if you come to believe and hitch your
> cart to a star. She is gentle when she nurses the clouds
> with her breast, but when calm has left her she runs on
> the seashore and throws her arms into the sky.
> In her eyes I see how two angels have come to stand
> at my shoulders: the pale, malicious angel of Irony, and
> the powerful, loving angel of Schizophrenia.

The startling opposition of Irony and Schizophrenia as two guardian angels who otherwise stand in total contrast with each other is extremely significant here. The consequence of such a confrontation would be the conclusion that Irony—this time considered as a subjective individual attitude and not an objective feature of reality—is the highest degree of reason, just as Schizophrenia represents the ultimate insanity. Man is faced with an alternative: he may either submit passively to the power of his own imagination, which embraces the world in an all-accepting ("loving") way, or find a weapon, both offensive and defensive, in his critical ("malicious") ability to distance himself from the world. In other words, it is insanity that "invites" man with the phrase "you will be happy if you come to believe"; I may add that irony offers him another chance: "you will be saved if you remain skeptical."

A similar—but interestingly modified—notion of irony is referred to in a third personification, included in the famous prose poem "From Mythology" (SP 38, M 93):

> First there was a god of night and tempest, a black
> idol without eyes, before whom they leaped, naked
> and smeared with blood. Later on, in the times of the
> republic, there were many gods with wives, children,
> creaking beds, and harmlessly exploding thunderbolts.

At the end only superstitious neurotics carried in their
pockets little statues of salt, representing the god of
irony. There was no greater god at that time.
    Then came the barbarians. They too valued highly
the little god of irony. They would crush it under their
heels and add it to their dishes.

There are several things in this meaning-laden poem that deserve
special attention. First of all, for the first time in Herbert's work
the problem of irony is situated along the axis of history, along the
"past-present" line so essential in Herbert's poetic philosophy. Second, the issue of historical evolution is adjoined here by other pairs
of opposed notions, in particular by the oppositions of Mediterranean tradition and barbarity, myth and experience, gods and humans, each of which we have already encountered in many other
of Herbert's poems. Irony occupies a special place within this set
of notions. It is all that remains from the Mediterranean myth—
remnants of divine transcendence, an individual "neurotic's" only
chance for spiritual self-defense. However, even though there is no
better chance, this one too can be brutally destroyed; in the eyes of
barbarians no transcendence whatsoever exists (including the transcendence of reason), since it simply does not fit into their system
of values, in which the only use for Attic salt is to "add it to their
dishes." The whole poem, then, is significant inasmuch as it offers
an example of irony raised, as it were, to the second power—an
ironic attitude to irony itself.

THE poet's overt and manifest references to the personified notion
of irony are perhaps one reason why the critics seem to be particularly sensitive to this question: among those who write on Herbert
there is probably no one who has failed at least to mention casually
that irony is the most distinguishing feature, almost the hallmark
of his poetry. But such remarks only contribute to the emergence
of another meaningless label, if no thought is given to the specific
sense of the term "irony" in Herbert's poetic method. And, in fact,
nearly no thought is given to this.[1] Apart from the penetrating,
although not always consistent and precise, essay by Jan Błoński,[2]
Herbert's critical bibliography does not include any work that approaches this problem head on—that, in other words, attempts to
answer the questions of what Herbert's irony actually is from the
point of view of rhetorical techniques, what are his particular

methods for using it in his poetry, where the possibilities of perceiving irony by the implied reader lie, what functions irony performs, and finally, where the boundaries of irony can be located,
that is, what values reside beyond the reach of irony in Herbert's
poetry.

The matter is difficult, to be sure. Many volumes have been filled
with theoretical reflection on various meanings of the very word
"irony" from both a historical and a contemporary perspective.[3] In
Herbert's case we are nearly always dealing with just one of the two
fundamental kinds of irony: with "being ironical" rather than
"seeing things as ironic," in other words with so-called verbal irony
rather than situational irony.[4] The personification of the kind of
irony characteristic of Herbert would be the god from the poem
"From Mythology" rather than the goddess from "The Altar."
True, situational irony is also to be encountered in Herbert's
poems, and is sometimes even introduced in the most open manner, by means of what the theoreticians of ironical rhetoric call a
"straightforward warning in the author's own voice."[5] For example, in the last sentence of the prose poem "Fotoplastikon"—"A
streetcar, an ironic transatlantic liner, rings for the dreamers"—it is
obvious that we are dealing with situational irony. The whole poem
speaks of people whose only chance to escape from everyday existence is their dreams about exotic travels. In this context, the irony,
signaled straightforwardly by the adjective "ironic," is obviously
produced by the situation itself. The appearance of an ordinary
streetcar is seen as ironic, and this objective fact does not result
from anybody's deliberate intent. Here again we encounter Herbert's typical unmasking confrontation between the world of
mythically exotic "heritage" and the world of empirically concrete
"disinheritance," but, in this rather atypical case, the confrontation
is due to an objective situation rather than to the author's creative
manipulation. If we tried to reduce "Fotoplastikon" to a simple
logical pattern, we would have to resort to the formulation "it is
ironic that . . ." rather than to the formulation "the fact that . . . is
presented with irony."

Such cases, however, are relatively rare. More characteristic of
Herbert are the countless occasions on which he resorts to verbal
irony, as a rule—though not always—leaving the reader no doubt
that something "is presented with irony," that somebody "is being
ironical." But the central question here is: *Who* is this "somebody"?
Who is the actual sender of the ironic message? When we come to
the conclusion that "he does not mean what he says" (which is a

simplified but basically accurate definition of verbal irony), are the one who "means" and the one who "says" always the same person? And if not, what is the nature of the distance between the two?

It is clear that we cannot approach these fundamental issues properly without considering Herbert's various characteristic methods for "manipulating the lyrical speaker,"[6] or, to be more precise, the various possible models of the relationship between the implied author and the speaker that occur in his poetry. This relationship can assume so many different forms that they would have to be presented as a continuous spectrum extending from the extreme of complete identification to that of total disidentification. In order to make this picture more schematic, I shall divide the continuum of possibilities into several basic categories. Polish descriptive poetics distinguishes among *liryka bezpośrednia* (direct lyricism), *liryka maski* (the lyricism of a mask), and *liryka roli* (the lyricism of a role).[7] These categories would serve our purposes excellently but for the fact that a literal translation of the Polish terms might be confusing. I shall replace them, then, by the terms "direct monologue," "persona monologue," and "dramatic monologue."

These three differ in the degree of distance between the implied author and the speaker. In a direct monologue (which is a broader notion than a "confessional monologue": what the speaker says does not necessarily have to be personal in character) we have—insofar as is possible in a work of literature—an identification of the speaker with the implied author. In the case of a persona monologue there appears an element of distance; the author has the speaker, his persona, "do his work for him." As is generally known, the notion of persona (whose psychological sense was popularized by Jung) in antiquity meant simply a theatrical mask.[8] A mask is not a complete disguise, though; the very term implies that the reader of a persona monologue has to be aware of both the similarity and the nonidentity of "the mask" (the speaker's personality) with "the face" (the implied author's personality, hidden behind the mask but nonetheless present and noticeable). Finally, in a dramatic monologue[9] the distance is at its greatest: the speaker is not only clearly not identical with the implied author; he cannot be even considered by any means that author's "disguise," *porte-parole*, or persona.

How do these three categories relate to the various forms of verbal irony, so profusely classified by theoreticians since ancient times? The modern classification, introduced by D. C. Muecke, seems to be the most useful and easy to handle. Muecke singled out four basic "modes of irony," distinguished by the increasing distance between the "ironist" and his "voice," "persona," or "character." The principle of distinction is precisely what interests us here. The trouble is that Muecke's four modes cannot possibly coincide with our scheme of three types of lyrical monologue. For example, a direct monologue would, as often as not, be a case of what he calls "impersonal irony" (characterized by "the absence of the ironist as a person; we have only his words"). But a direct monologue can also employ "self-disparaging irony," in which the ironist is present "as a person with certain characteristics."[10] Now, if some of the ironical narrator's characteristics make us believe that he is not so much a true representative as a disguise of the implied author—in other words, if the distance between the two is greater than it can possibly be in a direct monologue—we will have to speak of such self-disparaging irony as employed within the framework of a persona monologue. The same kind of monologue can, however, employ what Muecke calls "*ingénu* irony," where the distance is even more marked (we realize that the author knows more or better than the naive speaker employed by him) but we still should "see the ironist beneath the disguise": "the simpleton" still acts on behalf of "the ironist" despite all differences between them.[11] If, finally, the distance grows beyond any possible identification of these two personalities, the same *ingénu* irony can reveal itself in a dramatic monologue. The kind of irony that fits a dramatic monologue most tightly is Muecke's fourth mode, the so-called dramatized irony or irony of self-betrayal, in which "the ironist does not appear either as an impersonal voice or in any disguise," but instead "he simply arranges that the characters . . . expose themselves in their ironic predicament directly to the audience or reader."[12]

This complicated arrangement can be schematically presented as in the following list:

Modes of irony	Forms of monologue
impersonal irony	
	direct monologue
self-disparaging irony	
	persona monologue
ingénu irony	
	dramatic monologue
dramatized irony	

In the ensuing analysis of Herbert's uses of irony, I will not follow the natural order of increasing distance: after characterizing the two extremes, direct and dramatic monologues, I will finally come to the dissection of specific cases of persona monologue, whose various models in Herbert's poetry offer a particularly interesting set of problems.

The Direct Monologue

One of Herbert's most "direct" lyrics is his poem "Meditations on the National Problem."[13] There can be no doubt in the mind of the reader that the speaker of this poem, its lyrical "I," present in grammatical forms such as "I would like to know at last," and "frankly I don't know / I only note that . . . ," is virtually identical (as far as is possible in literature) with its implied author. To put it in a different way: we can assume that everything the poem's "I" says is at least congruent with the author's opinions (more exactly, with those of his opinions he chose to present in this particular poem). This is especially clear in the final part of the poem, where the openly expressed conclusions concerning the title problem are deliberately put "in a form of a last will / that it might be known." But even this apparently straightforward poem is not free from irony. Let us look at the initial fragment:

> The fact of using the same curses
> and similar love entreaties
> often leads to too-bold conclusions
> Sharing the same reading list in schools
> also should not be a sufficient premise
> to kill
> The same thing with the land
> (willows sandy road wheat field sky plus cirrus clouds)

Irony is signaled here by means of stylistic contrast: *ex definitione* irrational phenomena such as nationalism or chauvinism are discussed in a deliberately cool and precise, almost scientific style that appraises things from the point of view of their rational, logical justification. For example, the cautious sentence "Sharing the same reading list in schools / also should not be a sufficient premise / to kill," is a classic illustration of a particular form of irony called litotes or understatement—the speaker says *less* than the author's supposed real intent (we could reconstruct the latter as a hypothetical sentence: Sharing the same reading list in schools as a premise to kill those who had different lists is absurd). Classification according to traditional rhetoric is, however, not so important here; what is essential from our point of view is that even within this extremely personal, almost confessional (at least at the end) poem, Herbert is apparently unable to dispense with irony.

I must add that, as A. Alvarez once noted, irony in Herbert is, as a rule, a "two-edged weapon."[14] If we are to accept the traditional distinction according to which each use of irony involves three persons—the "ironist," his "listener," and his "victim"[15]—we can ask who actually is the "victim" in "Meditations on the National Problem." Is irony directed only against those who understand the title problem in the spirit of primitive nationalism and chauvinism? If the implied author's own stance consisted in the opposite attitude, in some kind of cosmopolitanism, then simple sarcasm would probably have sufficed as an instrument to discredit the "victim."[16] Irony is a much subtler instrument than sarcasm; and it is employed here because it has to serve a complex purpose of refutation of views that easily could (but should not) be confused with the author's own. As it is, Herbert's irony in this poem denounces both sides—both thoughtless jingoism and soulless cosmopolitanism. The lines about the "reading list" reveal the absurdity of chauvinist pigheadedness as well as the absurdity of the opposite extreme—the seemingly rationalistic, cool-headed negation of the meaningfulness of national ties. The conclusion expresses open disagreement with both positions at once; at this moment the distance between the speaker and the author fades away and there is no trace of irony left in the poem:

> thus finally in a form of a last will
> that it might be known:
> I used to rebel against it
> but I think this blood-stained knot
> should be the last
> to be torn
> by someone tearing himself free

While speaking of irony as signaled by stylistic contrast, I touched on the important problem of how irony can be recognized: in other words, the problem of, as W. C. Booth puts it, "clues to irony."[17] The rhetoric of irony as seen from this point of view is excellently illustrated in virtually every poem by Herbert. In each such case, the implied reader's role consists in discerning some hidden conflict, incongruity, or distance that is the clue to his realization of the ironic character of the poem. Following Booth's classification, let me quote a few examples of such clues, which reveal their presence in Herbert's direct monologues:

Known Error Proclaimed

In "A Tale," (H 30, M 44) we read:

> when singing [the poet] deeply believes
> that he advances the sunrise

Obviously enough, the person "listening" to the "ironist's" voice must see that belief as a blatant error. But who is the "victim" of Herbert's irony this time? Once again we see that Herbert does not use the weapon of irony to achieve a cheap triumph for common sense. These lines may be ironical toward "the poet" and his megalomaniac fantasies about his own omnipotence (the irony is additionally helped by the contrast between those fantasies and the character's nonheroic looks: "he cranes his long neck / his protruding Adam's apple / is like a clumsy finger on a wing of melody"), but the final stanza, in which irony disappears, restores the balance between the world of mythic illusion and the world of experience:

> what would the world be
> were it not filled with
> the incessant bustling of the poet
> among the birds and stones

Conflicts of Facts within the Work

In the case of this clue, we deal not with a conflict between our knowledge and the opinions expressed in a poem, but with apparent contradictions within the poem itself. In "How We Were Introduced" (H 97), one of his most autobiographical direct monologues, Herbert tells a story of his official literary initiation in the years of political "thaw." The guardians of culture, who are just setting the "spontaneous literary movement" into motion, are so protective toward young poets, they even arrange children's parties for them:

> there were other boys there
> also in short pants
> scrupulously shaven
> shuffling their feet

The incoherent image of poets both "in short pants" and "shaven," boys and grownups at the same time, is a simple example of a clue that leads to the discovery of irony in the poem. But the irony in this particular poem does not appear so simple when we try to determine which of its modes is represented here and who its "victim" is. The very use of the past tense in the narration, in other words, the distance in time between the moment of speaking and the events related (for example, the author's remembered first steps in the officially approved literary world) serves as the means of shifting toward the mode of "self-disparaging irony": not only the hypocrisy of the pseudoprotectors of literature but also the childish naiveté of the speaker himself becomes the victim of ironic unmasking.

Clashes of Styles

Herbert's poetry abounds in examples of this clue to irony: its use acquires a special ideological significance in situations where clashing styles are representative of certain opposed systems of values. Such is, for instance, the case when a style characteristic of the historical past, myth, and Mediterranean tradition is contrasted with a style that is distinctly modern and pedestrian.

> Jonah son of Amittai
> running away from a dangerous mission
> boarded a ship sailing
> from Joppa to Tarshish
>
> the well-known things happened
> great wind tempest
> the crew casts Jonah forth into the deep
> the sea ceases from her raging
> the foreseen fish comes swinging up

In these lines from "Jonah" (SP 40–41, M 94–95) there is an interplay of contrasts between biblical quotations and allusions ("the sea ceases from her raging" sounds even more archaic in the Polish original, *morze staje od burzenia swego*) and the casual and nonchalant manner of the modern speaker, who liberally employs not only colloquial speech but also some elements of a mass-media style ("running away from a dangerous mission" could be a snippet from a spy novel or a tabloid). The clash is deliberately planned (and is even more dramatic in the next part of the poem where "the modern Jonah . . . behaves more cleverly / than his biblical colleague"), since the point of the poem is the hiatus between two value systems, the impossibility of myth under present circumstances:

> the modern Jonah
> goes down like a stone
>
> . . . . .
>
> the parable
> applied to his head
> expires
> and the balm of the legend
> does not take to his flesh

This, however, does not mean that the realm of heritage is the exclusive victim of irony in this poem. It is precisely the poem's style that allows us to see the actual direction taken by the ironic assault. Significantly, in the end of the poem, just quoted, the speaker returns to the biblical and archaic style (which is again more discernible in the Polish original, particularly in the syntax or vocabulary of the final five lines), as if it symbolized an ultimate, more reliable point of support. As usual, Herbert's irony cuts both ways: often within a single poem irony can turn, subsequently or simultaneously, against the heritage of the past or myth as well as against the disinheritance of modern experience.

Conflicts of Belief

In this clue to irony the issue of the distance between the implied author and the speaker gains particular importance, since this is a case of a "conflict between the beliefs expressed and the beliefs we hold and suspect the author of holding."[18] In "The Substance" (H 100–101, C 27–28), Herbert introduces an opposition between the majority of people, "loving life," and the few heroes who do not hesitate to offer their lives for a cause—in other words, between the "living plasma" of society and its "beautiful dead":

> those perish
> who love beautiful words more than fat smells
> fortunately they are few

The key to understanding the poem properly is the question of whether the word "fortunately" is to be taken seriously. Is it an expression of views that are really the implied author's own? Is the poem, consequently, really an unequivocal proclamation in favor of Sancho Panza and against Don Quixote, in favor of Fortinbras and against Hamlet? How thoroughly concealed are the clues to irony in this poem is demonstrated by how often the critics have interpreted "The Substance" simplistically, as if the answers to these questions were affirmative.[19] In fact, that is a wrong interpretation—the word "fortunately" is obviously ironical. We know this, however, chiefly because our acquaintance with other poems by Herbert[20] has already made it possible for us to construct a portrait of the implied author of his poetry—a moralist unable to accept as his own philosophy the principle of survival at any cost. Within the poem, itself, though, there is almost nothing that would provide us with a sufficient clue to the irony: read as an isolated and anonymous text, "The Substance" could be easily understood as unequivocal praise for survivors. It could—at least until its final words:

> the nation endures
> and returning with full sacks from its routes of retreat
> builds triumphant arches
> for the beautiful dead

Here the discreet mention of "full sacks" makes the alert reader correct his previous line of interpretation. Now he has to see that the meaning of the poem is ironical; that the phrase "the nation endures" is much richer in various shades of emotion than, for instance, Carl Sandburg's optimistic "the people will live on."

To conclude this analysis of irony in Herbert's direct monologues, I must make one important remark. As the example of "The Substance" has just shown, it is necessary to bear in mind that Herbert's mechanisms of irony often operate by means of surprise, by misleading the reader only to open his eyes suddenly a moment later. The same principle makes its presence felt when it comes to assigning a monologue to one category or another. An excellent example of the effect of surprise in this respect is the poem

"Parable of the Russian Emigrés" (H 95, M 61). To all appearances, this is just a casual story about the Russian aristocrats, who escaped to Poland after the Revolution and soon fell victim to personal catastrophe or social degradation:

> after a couple of years
> only three of them were spoken about
> the one who went mad
> the one who hanged himself
> she to whom men used to come
>
> the rest lived out of the way
> slowly turning into dust

From the beginning of the poem we assume—there is no indication to the contrary—that we are dealing with a typical case of direct monologue, in other words, that the distance between the implied author and the speaker is minimal or none. The last part of the poem, however, brings a surprise. The last three lines, distinguished only by indentation, inform us that what we have heard thus far is actually a quotation of a story told by someone else:

> This parable is told by Nicholas
> who understands historical necessities
> in order to terrify me i.e. to convince me

From this moment on, moreover, we also understand that Nicholas, thus far the speaker, by no means advocates views to which the implied author could subscribe. We have every reason to believe that the latter by no means approves the notion of "historical necessities" (a transparent pseudonym for Marxist historical dialectics) and the resulting intellectual surrender to the so-called laws of progress. He is also by no means a supporter of the thesis that in order to "convince" it is enough to "terrify." Therefore, Nicholas has to be considered not only as nonidentical with the implied author but also as his outright ideological enemy. His arguments, seemingly made more appealing by being illustrated by the tragic fate of White émigrés (probably told, incidentally, to discourage the interlocutor from another kind of emigration, namely "internal emigration," withdrawal from public life in rejection of political subservience), are indeed "terrifying" but not necessarily "convincing." The irony—which can be discovered, if nowhere else, in the laconic "i.e." in the last line—cannot, under the circumstances, deny the truth of the story told, nor can it dismiss its tragic import; it can, however, serve as a defensive weapon against the intellectual and moral coercion used by advocates of "historical necessities."

The Dramatic Monologue

From the point of view of lyrical discourse, "Parable of the Russian Emigrés" is already quite close to the dramatic monologue, a technique that has flourished in Herbert's poetry especially since the phase of *Studium przedmiotu*. Anyone acquainted with his poetry is well aware that some of Herbert's most acclaimed poems—such as "Elegy of Fortinbras" and "The Return of the Proconsul"—owe their artistic success to their ingenious use of dramatic monologue.[21] In poems of that kind Herbert's irony is perhaps most exposed and manifest, although this overtness does not preclude ambiguity, which has often led to misinterpretation. Needless to say, Herbert has many predecessors in employing this particular kind of monologue within a lyrical work. The dramatic monologue and the phenomenon of, as Robert Langbaum has put it, "the poetry of experience,"[22] have a long and rich tradition in European literature. To confine ourselves solely to the post-Romantic epoch, it is enough to mention Browning and Cavafy as two—of course, very different—masters of that technique (and in fact Herbert seems to owe a great deal to Cavafy). The Polish reader cannot help recalling its native tradition as well, reaching back to Adam Mickiewicz and culminating, in our century, in some of the poems of Czeslaw Milosz.[23]

In Herbert's work, however, this technique appears in a slightly different context, as the dramatic monologue is only the extreme point on a scale of increasing distance between his implied author and his speakers. Such distance, as I have noted, exists even in his most "direct" and "personal" poems: between his direct and dramatic monologues there is, so to speak, only a quantitative difference. Nevertheless, there is one feature that places the dramatic monologue in a separate category. This is the fact that in the dramatic monologue the implied author and the speaker are distinctly and manifestly nonidentical as "persons" and personalities; moreover, there is an emphasis on the fundamental nonidentity of their opinions, systems of values, and so on. In other words, contrary to the persona monologue, the dramatic monologue *sensu stricto* occurs when there can be no doubt that the speaker does not represent the author in any relevant respect. "Dramatized irony," or the "irony of self-betrayal" serves precisely this purpose—the speaker (who is, at the same time, a dramatic character) must compromise himself in the eyes of the reader (even though he is not aware that he does so) and thus compromise or unmask a certain idea, attitude, or mentality that the speaker represents and the implied author questions.

In Herbert's poetry this goal is achieved by a variety of specific forms of "dramatized irony." I should first distinguish between two different types of dramatic speaker. The speaker can appear in a poem either as a specific character, usually a historical figure or a literary or mythical personage endowed with a name, biography, and other individual features, or as a less defined personality whose specific traits can be only inferred from his diction, assumed point of view, expressed opinions, or emotional reactions. One brilliant example of the latter solution is provided by "A Russian Tale" (H 174, M 75), which has to be quoted in full:

> The tsar our little father had grown old, very old.
> Now he could not even strangle a dove with his own
> hands. Sitting on his throne he was golden and frigid.
> Only his beard grew, down to the floor and farther.
>
> Then someone else ruled, it was not known who.
> Curious folk peeped into the palace through the windows but Krivonosov screened the windows with gibbets. Thus only the hanged saw anything.
>
> In the end the tsar our little father died for good.
> The bells rang and rang, yet they did not bring his
> body out. Our tsar had grown into the throne. The
> legs of the throne had become all mixed up with the
> legs of the tsar. His arm and the armrest were one. It
> was impossible to tear him loose. And to bury the tsar
> along with the golden throne—what a shame.

The speaker's specific use of language (repeating standard formulas like "the tsar our little father," and using syntax that, in the Polish original, sounds like a calque from Russian) and his attitude to what he is talking about (strangling doves—and perhaps not only doves—is apparently a favorite pastime of the monarch, which the speaker matter-of-factly accepts; the ominous Krivonosov is, for him, a well-known figure whose role does not have to be explained) reveal his personality, but in a relatively indirect way. Although we do not know his name, age, sex, biography, or social position, we can at least guess that he fully belongs to the epoch and the society of which he speaks. Thus, he represents a mentality that is obviously alien to the implied author's: in order to unmask that difference (in this case, in a comical rather than a moralistic way, although in the final analysis the issues at stake are quite weighty), Herbert makes the speaker compromise himself, perform an act of "self-betrayal." The serene or casual tone the speaker uses to relate the atrocities, palace intrigues, and slavish cult of a ruler signifies that, in fact, he accepts the despotic system in which he lives.

A more complex use of the same technique is exemplified by another well-known poem, "At the Gate of the Valley" (H 9, M 35). As the critic Jerzy Kwiatkowski has pointed out in his analysis of that poem, the clue to the irony is provided here mainly by the clash of styles, or perhaps the clash between style and subject.[24] The scenery of the Last Judgment is presented by a speaker who uses the style of a modern radio announcer, as if he were covering a soccer match or a May Day parade:

> but enough of these remarks
> let us lift our eyes
> to the throat of the valley
> from which comes a shout
>
> . . . . .
>
> it is we are told
> a cry of mothers from whom children are taken
> since as it turns out
> we shall be saved each one alone
>
> the guardian angels are unmoved
> and let us grant they have a hard job

Here, as in "A Russian Tale," the dramatic portrait of the speaker has to be reconstructed by the implied reader on the basis of the text alone, without any preestablished knowledge; the only clues are provided by the components of the speaker's own indirect self-characterization in the course of the poem. However, the problem of the "irony of self-betrayal" is much more complex here. Not only the superficial and insensitive mentality of the speaker is compromised, and not only the sphere of modern indifference and nihilism (of which that mentality is representative); the reality the speaker describes—the reality of myth—is also compromised, since the scenery of the Valley of Joshaphat reveals a distressing similarity to a concentration camp. In other words, both the realm of heritage condensed into myth (in this case, biblical eschatology) and the realm of modern disinheritance appear as equally cruel and inhuman. All the additional complications considered, the key to such vision is still provided by the technique of the dramatic monologue: the concept of the Last Judgment becomes unmasked, "betrays itself" only because of the way it is described by the "self-betraying" speaker.

Another type of dramatic monologue depends, as I have noted, on the construction of a speaker-character who is endowed with more specific and individual traits, such as a proper name and a role as a well-known historical figure or as a literary or mythical personage. Titles like "Elegy of Fortinbras," "Caligula" (P 54, C 49), and "The Divine Claudius" (R 41, CR 36) function as a way of introducing the dramatic speaker by name from the very beginning of a poem. Sometimes a poem of that kind is preceded, in a subtitle or even in a title, by a phrase reminding one of stage directions in drama: "Caligula speaks:" or "Damastes (Also Known As Procrustes) Speaks" (R 49, CR 44), which removes any potential doubts as to who delivers the monologue. Obviously, this type of dramatic speaker is an extreme instance of nonidentity with the implied author—from the initial indications it is self-evident that the speaker is at least physically nonidentical with the author, and the ensuing parts of the poem usually provide other evidence that the speaker cannot be considered even a persona or *porte-parole* for the author. Nevertheless, despite that unequivocal nonidentity, the mechanisms of ironic self-betrayal are subtle here as well and require a great deal of the reader's cooperation. The critic Janusz Sławiński, in his excellent analysis of "Elegy of Fortinbras," has already demonstrated that a full and proper reading of that poem—as a poem on an irresolvable conflict of two opposed attitudes—and an appreciation of its irony demand that the reader be knowledgeable in such arcane fields as the literary tradition of the funeral elegy, the rhetorical rules for constructing a eulogy for the dead, and the history of the Hamlet motif in literature.[25] Some other critics have "proved" inadvertently by their own analyses that to forsake this necessary knowledge means to misunderstand the problem of irony and to reduce the meaning of "Elegy of Fortinbras" to a few shallow banalities.[26]

Let us examine another instructive example. It might seem that ancient history knows no figure more compromised than Caligula. Contrary to the morally ambiguous and controversial personalities of, say, Fortinbras, Claudius the Divine, or the Roman official from "The Return of the Proconsul," Caligula seems an unequivocal villain and, as such, not a very promising object for all the finesse of "irony of self-betrayal." Yet Herbert's dramatized irony reaches deeper, under the surface of popular stereotypes. In his "Caligula" he lets the mad emperor speak, as if to offer him a chance to present his motives. In fact, the ironist does not try to make his job easier—the speaker, Caligula, presents his motives in a strikingly logical way:

> Incitatus was full of qualities
> he never gave speeches
> a stoic nature
>
> . . . . .
>
> he accepted the rank of consul indifferently
> he performed his duties excellently
> that is he didn't perform them at all

We are tempted to declare Caligula in the right: the best ruler—especially from the point of view of the oppressed—may be indeed the one who does not "perform [his duties] at all." It is only when we realize that Incitatus was actually a horse (a fact the speaker never tries to conceal) that Caligula's logic is revealed as insane. As always in Herbert's dramatic monologues, the "irony of self-betrayal" does not so much unmask the speaker himself (in this particular case it would be rather redundant) as the world view or value system he represents. In "Caligula" it is ultimately the nature of any despotism, which consists of drawing insanely logical conclusions from false assumptions, that becomes the principal target for ironic assault.

The Persona Monologue

As already discussed, the persona monologue falls in the middle on the spectrum of increasing distance between the implied author and his speaker; in other words, it forms the intermediate stage between direct and dramatic monologues. There are certain reasons, however, why the persona monologue deserves to be presented at the end of this chapter. First, in this type of monologue we encounter an exceptionally rich variety of specific forms of ironic distance and an exceptionally complicated network of relations between the implied author and his "mask" or persona.[27] Second, the development of Herbert's poetry seems increasingly to favor the persona monologue, to the point that he has made it the central narrative device of his latest work.[28]

By Herbert's latest phase, I mean specifically a large number of poems written since the early 1970s and forming—for the first time in Herbert's work—a distinct series,[29] united by the lyrical persona of Mr. Cogito. This character—always of the same name but with a seemingly fluid, hard-to-define personality—has apparently settled down in Herbert's poetry for good: his presence dominates not only the volume *Pan Cogito* (1974) but also the majority of poems in the most recent book, *Raport z oblężonego miasta* (1983). The Cartesian origin of the name[30] and some of the character's possible literary kin—Valéry's Monsieur Teste, Michaux's Plume, Pound's Mauberley, Eliot's Sweeney, Brecht's Herr K.—either are obvious or have already been pointed out by the critics.[31] What seems to remain unresolved is the extent to which Mr. Cogito speaks for the author, or, to put the question the other way around, the nature and extent of the distance (if any) between the implied author of the Mr. Cogito poems and Mr. Cogito himself.[32]

To answer this question, we must first gather and order the facts. First of all, we should realize that Mr. Cogito functions in Herbert's poems in at least two different ways—a point that is as important as it is rarely made by the critics. As one critic put it, Mr. Cogito is suspended "between an objectivized role and a projection of the consciousness of his creator."[33] To put it more simply: Mr. Cogito can be either the first-person speaker of a poem or its third-person character seen, as it were, from outside; he can either speak himself, or be spoken of.[34] To complicate the picture somewhat, Mr. Cogito can appear as either a "hidden speaker" (whose presence is only hinted at by some external signals, such as a title or epigraph) or an "overt speaker" (whose presence is clearly indicated in the text, for example by the monologue's grammatical forms). That accepted, we must acknowledge that the poems that revolve—in this or another way—around the figure of Mr. Cogito are not a homogeneous sequence. On the scale of increasing distance, the poems with Mr. Cogito as hidden speaker are nearest to the extreme of direct monologue, while those with Mr. Cogito as a third-person character (formally speaking, this would be a separate category) are closest to the extreme of the dramatic monologue. In all three variants, however different from one another as to the degree of distance, Mr. Cogito nonetheless remains the persona or lyrical mask of the implied author.[35]

What is meant here by a "hidden speaker" will become clearer when we examine poems like "Mr. Cogito Meditates on Suffering" (P 16, C 38), "Mr. Cogito and the Movement of Thoughts" (P 24, C 41), "Mr. Cogito Tells about the Temptation of Spinoza" (P 48, C 51), "What Mr. Cogito Thinks about Hell" (P 74, C 60), "Mr. Cogito on Virtue" (R 31, CR 26), or the famous "Envoy of Mr. Cogito" (P 78, C 79). In all these poems, the presence of Mr. Cogito—or, strictly speaking, the assurance that it is he who is speaking, meditating, telling, thinking, and so on—is evidenced by virtually nothing but the title. If not for the titles, we would probably read these poems as direct monologues that, to all intents and purposes, present positions and opinions approved by the author himself. In fact—and this may be a curious detail of literary history—at least some of these poems indeed were direct monologues before: in the literary press (and even in Herbert's *Poezje wybrane,* published in 1973 just before the appearance of *Pan Cogito*) they were printed in slightly different versions, without any mention of Mr. Cogito and under such titles as "On Suffering," "The Temptation of Spinoza," "The Envoy."[36] The introduction of Mr. Cogito in the titles might seem a strictly formal maneuver, then; it might be seen as forming *ex post* a poetic sequence out of poems that the author did not originally intend to form a sequence at all. But this is not merely a formal maneuver. The fact that Mr. Cogito is present, if only in the title, as a "hidden speaker" changes to a certain extent the impact of what is being said—the reader is compelled to modify his reading by the uncertain factor of potential distance between the implied author and the speaker. When we read, for instance, "What Mr. Cogito Thinks about Hell," we have to begin our attempt at understanding the poem by deciding first who Mr. Cogito actually is and whether his vision of Hell can be taken as corroborating the implied author's outlook.

This initial decision by the reader becomes even more crucial in the poems where Mr. Cogito appears as an "overt speaker," that is, where his opinions, confessions, accounts are presented in a first-person monologue. In poems like "Mr. Cogito Observes His Face in the Mirror" (P 5), "Mr. Cogito Considers the Difference between the Human Voice and the Voice of Nature" (P 36, C 46), "Mr. Cogito Laments the Smallness of Dreams" (P 40), "Prayer of Mr. Cogito—Traveler" (R 17, CR 12), to mention only a few, Herbert's persona is again introduced by name in the title, and, in addition, he functions within the poem itself as its first-person speaker. Naturally enough, in poems of this type, Mr. Cogito has, so to speak, more opportunity to present himself as an individual personality, with a more definite psychological profile, biography, intellectual background, and so on. Consequently, it is even more important that readers, in interpreting the poem, take into consideration the question of his relation to the implied author. Consider, for example, "Mr. Cogito Thinks about Returning to His Hometown" (P 14–15):

> If I went back there
> I probably wouldn't find
> a single shadow from my house
> nor the trees of my childhood
> nor the cross with the iron marker
> the bench where I whispered entreaties
> chestnuts and blood
> nor anything that belongs to us

The poem's title issues from the start a specific warning against a purely biographic interpretation, which most likely would be the reader's first impulse if the poem represented a typical, confessional, direct monologue. It is, of course, possible that for Herbert "hometown" signifies, among other things (as did "The Country" in the prose poem analyzed earlier) his native Lvov (with all the implications of the impossibility of any actual return, as suggested by the use of conditional in the first line). Nevertheless, the fact of the replacement of the direct monologue by the persona monologue makes the reader consider certain other, more universal meanings (for example, those connected with the existential opposition between childhood and adulthood, naiveté and consciousness, which play such an important role in all of Herbert's poetry). And besides, the remainder of the poem confirms this. Let us note the symbolic meaning, as already discussed, in the opposition between "white" and "gray," which is concealed here in the contrast between the "chalk circle" and the "ash":

> all that survived
> is a flagstone
> with a chalk circle
> I am standing in its center
> on one foot
> a moment before jumping
>
> I cannot grow up
> even though the years pass
> and above me
> planets and wars resound
>
> I stand in the center
> still as a monument
> on one foot
> before the jump into the ultimate
>
> the chalk circle turns rust-colored
> like old blood
> the mounds of ash around it
> grow
> up to the shoulders
> the mouth

The problem of distance becomes an issue of first importance in the third group of poems centered around the figure of Mr. Cogito—in those (incidentally, the most numerous) poems in which Herbert, as if tending toward the epic type of narration (in the sense of epic objectivization rather than epic story), introduces his persona as a third-person character. Obviously, in poems of this kind Mr. Cogito no longer functions as a speaker; even his point of view does not always provide the narration's perspective. The technique of third-person presentation is reserved for the poems in which there is maximum distance between the implied author and Mr. Cogito; still functioning as the former's persona or representative, Mr. Cogito is nonetheless subject to critical (or is it self-critical?) irony. Such a side view is necessary, for example, in a situation where Mr. Cogito's physical appearance is supposed to be a symbolic reflection of his spiritual split:

The left leg is normal
one might say optimistic
a little too short
boyish
smiling with muscles
with a well-modeled calf

the right one
is pitiful
thin
with two scars
one along the Achilles tendon
and the other oval-shaped
pinkish
a shameful reminder of running away

the left one
disposed to hopping
dancy
loving life too much
to get itself into trouble

the right one
nobly stiff
scoffing at danger

thus
on both legs
the left that can be compared to Sancho Panza
and the right
that resembles the knight errant
Mr. Cogito
walks
through the world
staggering slightly   ("On Mr. Cogito's Two Legs," P 7–8)

The artistic functions of the persona monologue and third-person presentation of a character become clearer in a comparison of this poem to another one with similar problematics: "The Substance," a poem already mentioned, from the early volume *Hermes, pies i gwiazda*. In "The Substance" an analogous conflict between two attitudes—a cowardly "love of life" and Quixotic heroism—is presented in social or national terms, with the silent majority on the one hand and a handful of the "beautiful dead" on the other. In the Mr. Cogito poem, the same conflict is placed within the individual, rendering it all the more insoluble, and, at the same time, it is "translated" into the language of appearance and anatomy. The grotesque character of this "translation" (the presentation of two spiritual categories as a pair of legs) and the outside point of view introduce the element of ironic distance, which finds particularly clear expression in the speaker's asides ("one could say optimistic," "pitiful") and his final sober observation of his character's "staggering."

From among the many other examples possible let me quote—in full—one more poem, "Mr. Cogito Reads the Newspaper" (P 22, C 39):

On the first page
a report of the killing of 120 soldiers

the war lasted a long time
you could get used to it

close alongside
the news of a sensational crime
with a portrait of the murderer

the eye of Mr. Cogito
slips indifferently
over the soldiers' hecatomb

to plunge with delight
into the description of everyday horror

a thirty-year-old farm labourer
under the stress of nervous depression
killed his wife
and two small children

it is described with precision
the course of the murder
the position of the bodies
and other details

for 120 dead
you search on a map in vain

too great a distance
covers them like a jungle

they don't speak to the imagination
there are too many of them

the numeral zero at the end
changes them into an abstraction

a subject for meditation:
the arithmetic of compassion

At first glance, the poem seems utterly transparent, devoid of symbolism, literal; a closer look, however, reveals that the interplay of
meanings, set into motion by the dynamically changing distance
between the implied author and the character, is quite complicated.
The gradual transformation of distance is the central poetic device
here. Beginning with fragments that seem to be direct quotations
of Mr. Cogito's thoughts ("the war lasted a long time / you could
get used to it") and continuing through the middle section, where
the distance suddenly increases and Mr. Cogito is seen from outside
and with clear irony (his eye "slips indifferently / over the soldiers'
hecatomb / to plunge with delight / into the description of everyday horror"), we finally arrive at the conclusion, where one of Mr.
Cogito's thoughts is again quoted and this disillusioned reflection
can be interpreted as both critical and self-critical. As a whole, the
poem is an exemplary instance of the technique of irony, by which
Herbert simultaneously identifies himself with and distances himself from Mr. Cogito; the distance is necessary for the poet to see
the character unflinchingly and objectively, while the identification
is needed for him to assume full responsibility for the character's
thoughts and actions.[37]

A thorough investigation of the poems employing Mr. Cogito
as a main personage (impossible here for reasons of space) would
lead to the conclusion that the "portrait" of Mr. Cogito, composed
of the numerous poems in which he appears (either as a hidden or
overt speaker or as a character), at least does not, despite all the
distance, contradict the "self-portrait" of the author implied in
Herbert's poetry. Like the implied author, Mr. Cogito is suspended
between two antinomically opposed worlds, between the realm of
heritage and the realm of disinheritance; like the author, he is not
able to fully identify with either of these two extremes. He belongs
to the disinherited world, he is a man-in-the-street, a reader of
newspapers, someone who visits shabby outskirts of the city; and
yet he "is a reflection of average consciousness but does not surrender to it"[38]—therefore he constantly seeks support in his memories
of mankind's lost heritage.[39] Thus, the same character can become
an object of a slightly grotesque description, as in "Two Legs of

Mr. Cogito," and can also be the speaker in the moralistic poem "The Envoy of Mr. Cogito": his personality does not thereby lose its consistency but rather gains in authenticity. Apart from other possible functions, irony—in this case, mainly "self-disparaging irony"—appears as a necessary means for revealing that insoluble contradiction, that crippled condition which makes Mr. Cogito "stagger slightly" while walking through the world.[40] Modern man's internal conflict, as represented by Mr. Cogito, is not re-solved by this—but at least it is made conscious, tamed by human thought, the thought that is symbolized by the character's name, hardly chosen at random.

FOUR

Imponderabilia

I HAVE stressed repeatedly that to achieve a full and deep understanding of the overwhelming majority of Herbert's poems one must penetrate the workings of irony in them. This is not enough, however. In the case of this particular poet, any inquiry into the problem of irony has little effect unless it includes consideration of two additional, closely connected issues: the *functions* and the *limits* of irony. In every kind of ironic moralism, the ultimate question is: For what purpose is the irony used? If it is not irony for irony's sake, what are its functions? Or, to view the same problem from another angle, what unquestionable, inviolable values remain after all the ironic unmaskings have taken place?

First, a few words about the functions of irony. They are many—and most of them are, of course, by no means only characteristic of Herbert's poetry. As it does in every bit of common speech or rhetorical text, irony (especially in the particular form of litotes, understatement)[1] can serve various purposes here too: it can help the poet tone down excessive pathos or emotion (in other words, it can serve as a defense against sentimentalism), avoid the unduly categorical (a defense against flat didacticism), lay bare certain insoluble contradictions and conflicts (a defense against partiality), and so on. Finally, and more universally, irony—considered as a signal from "ironist" to "listener" going over the head of its "victim"—can serve as a technique for making indirect and discreet reference to the value system shared by the poet and the reader.

This last function of irony in particular would seem the key to the specific character of irony in Herbert. It is extremely significant that in his poems we always encounter the same model (in different variants) for distributing roles among the ironist, the listener, and the victim: while the former two can, as a rule, be defined as underdogs, the victim of irony is actually a bully, stronger because of his social position, physical supremacy, psychological callousness, and so on. The only mainstay for the underdogs is the very values the bully violates; the only weapon left to them (since persuasion would have no effect, and simple sarcasm would be easy to disregard) is irony. As I have indicated, irony is usually a double-edged weapon, and it is double-edged in this situation as well: every ironic unmasking has self-irony as its reverse side. Every ironist has to be aware that his choice of irony as his weapon is imposed on him by his own weakness. At the same time, however, it is, paradoxically, a particularly efficient weapon—irony is the only method to make the bully compromise himself, to turn his superiority against him. If it is true that Herbert's poetry is, as one critic put it, a running "conversation with Caesar,"[2] and if we also assume that in such conversation the ironist is a "spokesman for the Republic"[3]—then irony seems a natural method of self-defense.[4] Herbert's poetry is self-ironic, in that it lays bare the shortcomings that do not allow Mr. Cogito to fulfill his desire of becoming Cato the Younger; but the edge of its irony is turned, first and foremost, against the bully, against Caesar.

Let us confine ourselves to a single example. In "Damastes (Also Known As Procrustes) Speaks"—one of Herbert's typical dramatic monologues—the mythological Attic bandit, known from the proverbial "procrustean bed," explains his intentions in the following way:

> in reality I was a scholar and social reformer
> my real passion was anthropometry
> I invented a bed with the measurements of a perfect
> man
> I compared the travellers I caught with this bed
> I couldn't avoid—I admit—stretching limbs cutting
> legs
> The patients died but the more there were who
> perished
> the more I was certain my research was right
> the goal was noble progress demands victims
>
> I longed to abolish the difference between the high and
> the low
> I wanted to give a single form to disgustingly varied
> humanity

I never stopped in my efforts to make people equal

. . . . .

I have the well-grounded hope others will continue my
    labor
and bring the task so boldly begun to its end
    (R 49, CR 44)

What we have here is a tyrant's self-portrait, drawn with the clear
intention of justifying his own deeds and whitewashing his image
for posterity; the voice of the ironist seems silent here. And yet the
irony in this particular poem proves more lethal than usual and the
self-indictment of the bully more than usually devastating. Why is
this so? The poem would lose all its ironic import if we read it in a
social and historical void. Apart from possessing an elementary
knowledge of mythology, the reader must share the implied author's knowledge of the basic ideological slogans of twentieth-
century totalitarian systems—their "scientific outlook," their
pseudo-egalitarianism, their belief in the superiority of "progress"
over any other value, their conviction that the ends justify the
means. Like the ironist, the listener must be someone who has
experienced what results from the actions of contemporary, Pro-
crustes-like "social reformers"; only then does the poem's speaker
clearly appear as an unequivocal victim of irony (in this case, irony
of self-betrayal). It is characteristic of the speaker's statements that
each of them can be objectively true (who knows, perhaps the bandit was not in fact sadistic and his "real passion was anthropome-
try"?); nevertheless, the value system they reflect obviously clashes
with the value system the ironist and the listener share. *They* know
very well that dreams of "a perfect man" ultimately result in the
use of brute force against real people who never come up to the
ideal; *they* know that progress should not come at the cost of human life, that equality should not mean brutal leveling. Moreover,
Damastes' logic does not accord with the logic of either the ironist
or the listener (that is, the implied author or the implied reader).
The statement "progress demands victims," for instance, would
not be so devastatingly ironic in relation to the speaker, if not for
the fact that, in the context of the whole poem, it is in fact the final
segment of a syllogism—"Every kind of progress brings victims;
my activity brought victims; therefore, my activity equalled progress"—an obvious abuse of logic.[5]

Irony as self-defense and defense of the underdog is specifically Herbertian; he has always been less interested in the victors and winners than in defeated individuals, defeated civilizations—as the title of one of his poems puts it, "Those Who Lost" (P 39).[6] This definition becomes even more precise if we place Herbert's method among the historically known forms of irony. These can be visualized as a panorama of attitudes extending between two extremes: Socratic irony and Romantic irony.[7] Socratic irony, treated as a model notion, can be considered a didactic means for inculcating a philosophy based on rational and stable values; from the point of view of rhetoric, the peculiar feature of the Socratic method lies in its combining the listener and the victim in one person; in the course of the dialogue, the ironist makes the listener a victim of irony and makes him realize this in order to open his eyes to his own error. Romantic irony—again, treated as a model notion—is based on the opposite ideological assumptions: it is principally the artistic result of the conviction that the world is unstable and irrational by its nature. Accordingly, from the point of view of rhetoric, Romantic irony, devoid of any didactic intent, makes no clear distribution of roles: the victim here is, as a matter of fact, the entire world, including the listener and the ironist himself.[8]

Set against these two extreme attitudes, Herbert's irony falls somewhere in the middle. Despite Herbert's frequent allusions that declare his solidarity with Socrates as an archetypal independent intellectual opposed to the power of the state and the power of public opinion,[9] the irony in his poetry is not in fact identical with Socratic irony. The internal contradiction between being loyal to the heritage of myth and belonging to the disinherited world of experience forces Herbert's implied author to maintain an uneasy balance between irrational and rational visions of the world—for a modern Socrates, Herbert is not enough of a teacher, not sure enough that his own logic is faultless or that all phenomena are explainable.[10] At the opposite extreme, the idea of Romantic irony, although also seemingly close to Herbert's work because of its elements of self-irony and disillusionment (that is, its unmasking of the essence hidden beneath appearances, with a constant assumption that—as in "Wooden Die"—this essence is itself nothing but appearance), is, at the same time, alien to him because of its fundamental philosophical relativism.[11] To put it briefly, Herbert's irony is too self-ironic to be Socratic irony, and too antirelativistic to be Romantic irony.[12]

THE consideration of Herbert's irony as suspended between the Romantic and the Socratic extremes leads us at last toward the exceptionally important problem of *the limits of irony*. As opposed to the work of typical Romantic ironists, for whom virtually anything could be unmasked and questioned, Herbert's poetry is characterized by the presence of certain imponderabilia, which irony cannot impair and does not even attempt to touch. I have already noted that, despite Herbert's dislike for didacticism and moralizing, his work does include poems in which the implied author's "own" voice breaks through all the ironic masks and disguises and in which certain values of the human world are unequivocally declared to be untouchable. If they are not absolutely untouchable, then at least they must not be questioned hastily and without due consideration. Recall the ending of "Meditations on the National Problem" (SP 48):

> I used to rebel against it
> but I think this blood-stained knot
> should be *the last*
> to be torn
> by someone tearing himself free

What are those untouchable values? This question brings us once again to a problem central to Herbert's poetry—that of the opposition between the realm of heritage and the realm of disinheritance. I have noted that insofar as Herbert accepts the state of disinheritance on empirical grounds (as if to say: such is objective reality and there is no reason why I should pretend that it is otherwise), he disapproves of it on ethical grounds (as if to say: this is not the reality I have chosen for myself, and there is no reason why I should pretend that I accept it). In other words, in his poetry the feeling of the irrevocability of disinheritance coexists with an equally strong sense of unity with the lost heritage. I have already documented this with a great many examples. But more needs to be said here: Herbert also states that even though disinheritance is irrevocable, there exist, paradoxically, certain values from which one *must not* let oneself be disinherited: values that man has been deprived of and that, at the same time, he cannot renounce since renouncing them would mean the loss of human identity.

One could say, then, that Herbert's poetry is based on a fundamental, deep-seated paradox: a sober recognition of the situation of contemporary man, constantly contradicted by a dramatic gesture of dissent from that situation. Let me first add a few details to Herbert's diagnosis. In its early phase, his poetry was dominated by the obsessional motif of "emptiness" or "void" (which sometimes, in other contexts, also appears as "silence," "absence" or other words with a negative meaning)—the "emptiness" left in today's world by the old values. Here are a few examples from *Struna światła:*

> Home . . .
> A square of *empty* space
> under an *absent* star   ("Home," SS6)

> Above my head
> *empty* like the air's brow
> a man's silhouette made from black paper
>   ("Three Poems from Memory," SS 8)

> Now the lips of the Poet
> are an *empty* horizon   ("Three Poems from Memory," SS 12)

> Your words' futility like an echo's shadow
> and the wind in the rooms of *empty* stanzas
>   ("To the Dead Poets," SS 13)

> The Poet fights his own shadow
> The Poet cries like a bird in the *void*   ("On Troy," SS 27)

These few quotations suffice to show that emptiness is attributed both to the outside world and to the psyche: it fills the surrounding reality (that is, the world after the annihilation of human values) as well as the "Poet" himself (who does not know how to react to that annihilation). Still, the "empty stanzas" and "silence" are not the Poet's only possible response. I will return to this problem when analyzing the aesthetic consequences of Herbert's ethics; it is, however, worth grasping at this point that, faced with such a fundamental alternative, the writer chooses a paradoxical and—at least seemingly—irrational solution. His decision is condensed, as it were, into the laconic phrase "And nonetheless" from the poem "Priest": *in spite of* being disinherited from values, in spite of the symbolic decapitation of a deity, in spite of his own helplessness, the poet-priest *nonetheless* continues his old ritual:

I impotent priest
who lifting up my hands
know that from this neither rain nor locust
neither harvest nor thunderstorm

. . . . .

—And nonetheless
I raise up eyes and hands
I raise up song

And I know that the sacrificial smoke
drifting into a cold sky
braids a pigtail for a deity
without a head   (SS 31–32, M 23)

Even in these early poems, however, Herbert's ethical diagnosis undergoes dramatic complications. The emptiness of the world that survived annihilation is not only being filled with individual "faithfulness," "loyalty" or "fidelity" (*wierność*)—seemingly absurd and irrational—to the old heritage of values. (This heritage is personified, incidentally, not merely by allegorical deities but, even more often, by quite realistic figures of the war dead; "fidelity" is identified with an obligation to remember them and their sacrifice.) The emptiness is also being filled with "life," "a new life" spread by the people who heed the prosaic voice of their instinct for self-preservation. A clash of these two notions and attitudes occurs, still in slightly allegorical form, in the early poem "Fortune-telling," which describes a palm with a "life line" and a "line of fidelity":

Here is the life line Look it races like an arrow
the horizon of five fingers brightened by its stream
which surges forth overthrowing obstacles
and nothing is more beautiful more powerful
than this striving forward

How helpless compared to it is the line of fidelity
like a cry in the night a river in the desert
conceived in the sand and perishing in the sand
(SS 76, M 29)

In the poems published during the next years this enigmatic opposition acquires content that is historically and socially more specific. In poems such as "The Substance" and, particularly, "Prologue" and "Awakening" (all mentioned earlier), the poet speaks of "a new life" that is tempting in its apparent accessibility ("and a new life was unrolling at our feet," N 12, M 132), while at the same time it conceals a basic danger. For, if one wants to enter the "stream" of a new life that "surges forth," one must first forget, rid oneself of fidelity, reconcile oneself to being disinherited from the old value system. It is significant that "a new life" holds all the trump cards, so to speak. For example, the "new life" appears fully consistent with the order of nature; this is why the Chorus in "Prologue" refers to this argument while encouraging the hero:

> Throw away memories. Burn remembrance and enter
>   the stream of a new life.
> There is only earth. One earth and the seasons of the
>   year are over it.   (N 8, C 21)

It is also why the resisting hero defines his attitude as: "I flow upstream."[13] While in accordance with the order of things in nature, the acceptance of "a new life" appears inconsistent with the ethical order, which had provided a basis for the heritage, lost but still referred to.[14] Herbert chooses fidelity. This is, *nota bene,* the point where he parts company with stoicism. The identification of virtue and nature, the founding of an ethical system on the principle of concordance with nature, so obvious for the Stoics, is unacceptable to Herbert.[15] Even though one of his poems is a dialogue with Marcus Aurelius, that philosopher's opinion—"Naught that is evil can be in harmony with Nature"[16]—has nothing in common with Herbert's poetry.

Clearly, in poems like "Awakening" or "Prologue" the notion of "a new life" carries specific historical connotations: apart from other possible meanings, it is connected to the situation of Polish intellectuals after 1944, when "the horror subsided the floodlights went out" and "we discovered that we were on a rubbish-heap in very strange poses" (N 12, M 132). The keenness of perception, characteristic of Herbert as an observer of modern times, is evident in the fact that his ethical diagnosis, while constantly based on the same fundamental antinomies, has nonetheless undergone certain significant modifications as social attitudes evolved in the course of history. In Herbert's more recent poems the opposition between fidelity and the "instinct of life" carries a slightly different meaning, and the centers of gravity seem to have shifted. Those for whom survival means everything are defined less ambiguously now, as ethical relativists or even nihilists; in more and more of his poems his diagnosis is primarily concerned with the widespread dissolution of value systems, the banalization of evil, the fading of threshold situations[17] in which contemporary man could define himself in moral terms, and the lack of transcendental mainstays toward which he could orient himself.[18] Emptiness, the notion that in Herbert's early poems was still a bit vague, now acquires new appearances and meanings. Perhaps most characteristic from this point of view—although similar motifs appeared in his earlier poetry—is the entire sequence of Mr. Cogito poems, where the problem of the decay of values, "spiritual pigmyism" and nihilism[19] becomes a central issue. After all, the hero of the sequence is a man who, despite all the self-ironic distance, still remains the implied author's persona—a man, then, for whom the world of the old values is still very much alive. However, even in his case ethical choices and decisions are somewhat dwarfed and trivialized, marked by the deep-rooted impossibility of continuing the traditional notion of tragedy. "The Abyss of Mr. Cogito," for instance:

> is not the abyss of Pascal
> is not the abyss of Dostoievski
> it is an abyss
> by Mr. Cogito's standards
>
> its characteristic feature
> is neither bottomlessness
> nor the inspiring of horror
>
> .   .   .   .   .
>
> onerous as eczema
> devoted as a dog
> too shallow to engulf
> the head arms and legs   (P 18)

In "The Monster of Mr. Cogito," not only the choice between good and evil but also the evil itself becomes analogically dissolved or blurred. Even if Mr. Cogito desires to be a modern Saint George, he finds himself in a baffling situation in which there is no dragon he could fight:

> the monster of Mr. Cogito
> has no measurements
>
> it is difficult to describe
> escapes definition

it is like an immense depression
spread out over the country

it can't be pierced
with a pen
with an argument
or spear

were it not for its suffocating weight
and the death it sends down
one would think
it is the hallucination
of a sick imagination

but it exists
for certain it exists

like carbon monoxide it fills
houses temples markets

poisons wells
destroys the structures of the mind
covers bread with mold

the proof of the existence of the monster
is its victims

it is not direct proof
but sufficient   (R 44–45, CR 39–40)

Mr. Cogito, who will not yield to "suffocation from formlessness," decides, in the second part of the poem, to take up a seemingly absurd fight with an invisible enemy, despite good advice from "reasonable people" who:

say
we can live together
with the monster

we only have to avoid
sudden movements
sudden speech

.   .   .   .   .

listen to wise Nature
recommending mimicry

that we breathe shallowly
pretend we aren't there   (R 45–46, CR 40–41)

But, Mr. Cogito is, despite everything, an exception: he "does not want a life of make-believe" (R 46, CR 41). Apart from him, in the overwhelming majority of cases, "suffocation from formlessness" remains a typical and essential feature of the modern world—the world disinherited of values. This kind of diagnosis seems to be the final conclusion of the enigmatic prose poem "The Missing Knot" (N 41, C 16):

> Clytemnestra opens the window, looks at herself in the glass to put on her new hat. Agamemnon stands in the vestibule, lights a cigarette, and waits for his wife. Aegisthus comes in at the main door. He doesn't know that Agamemnon returned home last night. They meet on the stairs. Clytemnestra suggests that they go to the theatre. From now on they will be going out a lot together.
> Electra works in the cooperative. Orestes studies pharmacology. Soon he'll marry his careless classmate with the pale complexion and eyes continually filled with tears.

At first glance, nothing really happens in this poem—but that, precisely, is its message. Agamemnon will not be murdered and avenged, Clytemnestra and Aegisthus will live out their banal lives and die natural deaths, Orestes and Electra will not become the heroes of any tragedy. What in the myth acquired the sharp outlines of tragic alternatives and the moral evaluation of human actions is here dissolved in an atmosphere of "suffocation from formlessness" where "the knot" is "missing." ("The missing knot" has at least two senses: it refers to both the lack of genuine connections between characters and the lack of threshold, "knotted" situations, in which fate would force the characters to make dramatic decisions.) Evil is banalized, fate is trivialized into blind chance (the carelessness of Orestes' classmate—Hermione, according to myth—most probably means that she has inadvertently become pregnant); myth transferred to our times loses its tragic dimension (the characters, removed from the tragic stage, only "go to the theatre") and in fact loses all meaning—it is no longer a statement about the world but merely a mosaic of incoherent facts.

An analogous process occurs in the poem "Inner Voice" (SP 66–67, M 113–114), which is yet another of Herbert's indirect polemics against stoicism. We might identify the title notion, which appears to be a reference to the ancient concept of *daimonion,* with spiritual harmony and a clear sense of choice between opposing values. After all, Diogenes Laertius wrote about daimonion: "And this very thing constitutes the virtue of the happy man and the smooth current of life, when all actions promote the harmony of the spirit dwelling in the individual man with the will of him who orders the universe."[20] In Herbert's poem, the "spirit dwelling in the individual man" behaves in quite a peculiar way. This excellent poem has to be quoted in full:

My inner voice
has nothing to advise
has nothing to warn against

does not say either yes
or no

is barely audible
and almost inarticulate

even if you bend way down
you hear only syllables
stripped of all meaning

I try not to drown him out
I deal with him civilly

I pretend to treat him as an equal
and that what he says is of great consequence

sometimes I even
try to engage him in conversation
—you know yesterday I refused
I've never done such a thing
I wouldn't now either

—glu-glu

—so you think
I did right

—ga-go-gi

I am glad we agree

—ma-a

—and now take a rest
we'll talk again tomorrow

he is no use to me
I could forget about him

I have no hope
a little regret
when he lies there
covered with pity
breathes heavily
opens his mouth
and tries to lift up
his inert head

The "inner voice," the daimonion of Socrates and the Stoics, is degraded here into an idiot's mumble, just as in "The Missing Knot" myth is degraded into an assortment of meaningless facts. What is most significant, however, is that "Inner Voice" is by no means an example of the dramatic monologue—there is no essential distance here between the speaker and the implied author, and we can assume that their positions are close to each other. The character-speaker is, then, not a nihilist who "could forget about" the dictates of his conscience simply because he does not care about moral principles in the first place. On the contrary, the character's statements make us conclude that he is an anachronistically *decent* individual, who plays it straight when faced with moral alternatives. The reason he does so, however, is not that he is impelled in that direction by some transcendent sanction, by "the will of him who orders the universe," which would manifest itself through the dictates of conscience; rather, the choice of a line of conduct appears to the speaker as a matter of consistency, a matter of—I have to use that word again—*fidelity* to the principles once considered as right ("I've never done such a thing / I wouldn't now either"). Even though he can no longer find support in any inner daimonion or external moral code, this character—a prototype of Mr. Cogito—is another one who does not want to suffocate from formlessness.

THUS far, I have been concerned mainly with Herbert's ethical diagnosis of the contemporary world of disinheritance. While aware of the threat stemming from the dissolution of values, the suffocation from formlessness, and the ethical void, the poet also opposes something to it. In his view, the greater the threat, the more urgent the necessity of remaining faithful to certain basic values that make us human—the values for which one of the Mr. Cogito poems proposes an all-encompassing name, "an upright attitude." Let us focus for a moment on this particular poem, one of Herbert's most vocal manifestoes of his ethics. "Mr. Cogito on Upright Attitudes" (P 75–77, C 64–66) refers to our times in an indirect, circuitous way, by using historical disguise. As the first line informs us, the action takes place "In Utica," that is, in the city that—as the reader is supposed to know—in 46 B.C. was one of Pompeius's last outposts of resistance against Caesar's troops. The implied situation is, then, a clash between the defenders of the republic and a dictator; however, what becomes the chief subject of the poem is not that conflict but rather a phenomenon described once before in Cavafy's famous poem "Waiting for Barbarians"—the defenders' moral capitulation, which occurs even before the actual surrender to the enemy:

> in town an epidemic broke out
> of the instinct of self-preservation
>
> . . . . . .
>
> the citizens
> don't want to defend themselves
> they are attending accelerated courses
> on falling to the knees

Placed in this historical situation, Mr. Cogito refuses to participate in "falling to the knees"; "like Cato the Younger / see in the *Lives*," he intends to persevere in his hopeless resistance to the bitter end. The second part of the poem is based on a subtle play on words and expressions connected semantically with vertical body positions;[21] Herbert lays bare this particular meaning by exposing the literal sense of the hackneyed phrase *stanąć na wysokości sytuacji* (to stand up to the situation), but he also introduces it more directly in speaking of "position" and "gesture":

> Mr. Cogito
> would like to stand
> up to the situation
>
> which means
> to look fate
> straight in the eyes

. . . . .

> little remained for him
> in fact only
> the choice of position
> in which he wants to die
>
> the choice of a gesture
> choice of a last word
> this is why he doesn't go
> to bed
> in order to avoid
> suffocation in sleep

In the poem's final lines, the already-introduced ambiguity of the phrase "to stand up to the situation" is once again referred to and ironically explicated:

> to the end he would like
> to stand up to the situation
>
> fate looks him in the eyes
> in the place where there was
> his head

The gesture of refusing to capitulate allows Mr. Cogito to "stand up to the situation" but at the same time it sentences him to physical annihilation. Let us also note a peculiar identification of "situation" and "fate": "to stand up to the situation" is precisely the same as to look, face to face, into the eyes of fate. This equation has two sides. On the one hand, it means that modern man must view fate, once mysterious and god-sent, as degraded to an ordinary "situation," a trivial coincidence; on the other hand, such "situations" are also thereby promoted to the rank of "fate," shown as something irreversible and objective. As a consequence of the latter side of the equation, a choice of a "position" or "gesture" will almost certainly have no impact on the actual development of the "situation," will not change it in the true sense of the word—nevertheless, by assuming an upright attitude and remaining vigilant, one at least avoids "suffocation in sleep," suffocation from formlessness and one's own unconsciousness. Similarly, in one of Herbert's most recent poems, "Report from the Besieged City" (R 81–82, CR 76–78)[22] written under martial law in Poland, the defenders' defeat is of less significance than the fact that their resistance alone was enough to save moral values:

> cemeteries grow larger the number of defenders
>   shrinks
> but the defense continues and will last to the end
> and even if the City falls and one of us survives
> he will carry the City inside him on the roads of exile
> he will be the City
>
> we look at the face of hunger the face of fire the face of
>   death
> and the worst of them all—the face of treason
>
> and only our dreams have not been humiliated

These are statements of enormous importance for the ethical message in the whole of Herbert's poetry. His ethics, as well as his poetic philosophy in general, is based on an unresolvable contradiction, an irremovable paradox. On the one hand, it is only the upright attitude, the refusal to participate in self-captivation, lies, and treason, that can save human dignity; if we accept this assumption, we must not consider such an attitude folly but the only way out and, in a sense, as rational behavior. On the other hand, there is absolutely no guarantee that such an attitude will bring any "actual" result; on the contrary, it is more likely, and indeed quite certain in most cases, that an upright attitude only makes decapitation easier. Such is the meaning of the last lines of the Utica poem, or of the ending of "The Power of Taste" (R 76, CR 70):

> to get out to make a wry face draw out a sneer
> even if for this the precious capital of the body the
>   head must fall

This kind of contradiction, intrinsically tragic, no longer in fact has much in common with the Stoics' ideal of *ataraxia*; the phrase "to stand up to the situation," as Herbert understands it, can even be considered an ironic comment on the maxim of Marcus Aurelius: "Adapt thyself to the things amidst which thy lot has been cast."[23] Not only is there no convergence between the notion of moral salvation and that of physical survival, but, in most situations, there is downright opposition—an opposition analogous to that between "the line of fidelity" and "the life line," between "the beautiful dead" and those who "love life." A similar tragic and paradoxical message is carried by the famous "The Envoy of Mr. Cogito" (P 78–79, C 79–80), which at present is certainly one of few genuinely well-known poems in modern Polish poetry. "Envoy" is another one of Herbert's ethical manifestoes, but it is no less complex and internally at odds than the other poems of this kind, a fact that seems to be overlooked even by otherwise penetrating critics who, as a rule, read the poem as an unequivocal program of "Stoic ethics" and "moral equilibrium."[24] A peculiar equilibrium indeed: here, virtually every exhortation of Mr. Cogito is immediately countered by a sharply contrasted, merciless warning; his conviction of the unconditional obligation to remain "faithful" to the heritage of moral values and to retain an "upright" attitude clashes constantly with his conviction of the equally unconditional inevitability of physical defeat. Let us read the poem differently from the way it is usually read, emphasizing those formulations which warn the reader of the ultimate futility of the "upright attitude" while, at the same time, paradoxically leaving intact the strength of the final call to "be faithful" to that attitude:

> Go where those others went to the dark boundary
> for the golden fleece of *nothingness* your last prize
>
> go upright among those who are on their knees
> among those with their backs turned and those toppled
>   in the dust
>
> *you were saved not in order to live*
> you have little time you must give testimony
>
> . . . . .
>
> and let your *helpless* Anger be like the sea
> whenever you hear the voice of the insulted and beaten
>
> let your sister Scorn not leave you
> for the informers executioners cowards—*they will win*
> they will go to *your funeral* and with relief will throw a
>   lump of earth
> the woodborer will write your smoothed-over
>   biography
>
> . . . . .
>
> repeat old incantations of humanity fables and legends
> because this is how you will attain the good *you will*
>   *not attain*

repeat great words repeat them stubbornly
like those crossing the desert who *perished* in the sand

and they will reward you with what they have at hand
with the whip of laughter with murder on a garbage heap
go because only in this way will you be admitted to the
    company *of cold skulls*
to the company of your ancestors: Gilgamesh Hector
    Roland
the defenders of the kingdom without limit and the *city*
    of ashes

Be faithful Go

From the point of view of practical rhetoric, this poem could seem absurd: it encourages only to immediately discourage, points out an obligation only to warn that its fulfillment would mean ridicule, defeat, annihilation. If there is any key to this apparent contradiction, it is hidden in the sentence "you were saved not in order to live"—the sentence that not only reveals the ambiguity of the word *ocalenie* (which means both survival and salvation) but also underscores the dual nature of man, for whom survival and salvation are by no means equal. Even though the latter is undoubtedly more important, this fact does not mean that the question of physical survival can be dismissed or forgotten; on the contrary, only those who are aware of danger can be heroic. As usual, the implied author remains—even in such a direct message as "Envoy"—suspended between the sphere of heritage and the sphere of disinheritance; not reconciled to being dispossessed of values, he nonetheless does not shut his eyes to the fact that the world around him has to a great extent reconciled itself to that dispossession. Hence, Mr. Cogito is a solitary hero: the cost of his refusal to surrender is that he must accept the prospect that his isolated attitudes and actions will meet defeat. This seems confirmed by the poem "Mr. Cogito on Virtue," (R 31–32, CR 26–27), where it is the word "virtue" (in the ancient sense of *virtus*) that becomes a synonym for the upright attitude. The choice of the word is no accident; the Polish word *cnota,* which also entails some connotations of sexual innocence, spinsterhood, and so on, and which sounds definitely old-fashioned, thus seems to invite sarcastic unmasking:

It is not at all strange
she isn't the bride
of real men

of generals
athletes of power
despots

through the ages she follows them
this tearful old maid
in a dreadful hat from the Salvation Army
she reprimands them

she drags out of the junkroom
a portrait of Socrates
a little cross molded from bread
old words

—while marvelous life reverberates all around
ruddy as a slaughterhouse at dawn

As we read the lines consecutively, however, it becomes increasingly obvious that the sarcasm is in fact irony, and that its victim is by no means the title notion of "virtue." Mr. Cogito, the hidden speaker of this poem, does not, after all, express his own (or the author's) opinions here, but experimentally assumes the viewpoint of "real men," or at least those who consider themselves as such—the "athletes of power" who believe only in the argument of brute force. This point of view is gradually compromised in the course of the poem, as its primitiveness is laid bare through the very logic of the argument, the construction of metaphors. The poem's implied reader is supposed to be unable to accept the opinion that it is "generals" and "despots" who are "real men," that "a slaughterhouse at dawn," of all things, can be a symbol of "marvelous life," and so forth. Therefore, in the ensuing part of the poem, even though the surface line of reasoning moves with increasing brutality toward ridiculing and repudiating "virtue," the reader gradually identifies himself with that notion and the value it signifies:

if she took care of herself
looked presentable
like Liz Taylor
or the Goddess of Victory

but an odor of mothballs
wafts from her
she compresses her lips
repeats a great—No

unbearable in her stubbornness
ridiculous as a scarecrow

as the dream of an anarchist
as the lives of the saints

Virtue is, thus, not only—in the trivial and practical sense—
fruitless and unprofitable, burdened with the "curse of virtue" or
the "solidarity between virtue and defeat," on which Herbert's
teacher Henryk Elzenberg wrote in his brilliant essay (in the 1940s)
on the defeat of Brutus.[25] Virtue is also unattractive, anachronistic,
ridiculous. Herbert seems to do his best, as if to spite himself, to
deprive his moral message of any persuasive force, anything attrac-
tive, any hope of success. To put it differently: his ethical system
and his persistent repeating of "great words" are not backed by any
pragmatic premise.[26] The moral message is not supported, either,
by any external sanction, any authority, any decalogue or code. All
that remains is a bare ethical imperative, a conviction that *one must
do it this way.*[27] The philosophical sources of this kind of ethics are
difficult to pinpoint precisely; the critics have probably been right
to interpret it as an eclectic union of lines of thought from the Stoic,
Christian, and Kantist traditions,[28] all individual differences not-
withstanding. Speaking in jest, one could view Herbert's ethical
system as an elaboration of a precept often used by the older poet
Antoni Słonimski: If you don't know how to behave in a particular
situation, behave decently just to be on the safe side.[29] Jests aside,
Herbert's system has undoubtedly much in common with Joseph
Conrad's ethics founded on the notion of individual responsibility
that is dictated not by any external authority (as we know, in Herbert's poetic world the figure of the authoritative Father has re-
ceded, as has childhood itself, into the irretrievable past) but by the
simple sense of commitment resulting from the very fact of belonging to the human species. This line of ethical reasoning seems
to have a particularly interesting and multifaceted tradition in today's Poland, and Herbert's poetry is an extremely important but
not a unique example of this trend. Suffice it to mention, on the
one hand, the intellectual tendency initiated by Leszek Kołakowski
in his essay "Ethics without a Code,"[30] and on the other the stim-
ulating reflections of Jan Józef Szczepański on the "Conradian situation," seen by him as "an imperative, undisputable ONE MUST DO
IT THIS WAY—the only illumination that throws light on our risky
paths." If, simplifying things of course, we also note that the same
point was reached by those three authors in the way of overcoming
very different philosophical traditions—the Marxist, the Christian,

and the Stoic—the fact that they ended up close to each other will appear as even more significant. Herbert, in any event, would certainly agree with Szczepański that Conrad was "deeply convinced of the pointlessness of any search for ultimate truths and, as a consequence, saw the essential meaning of life in the salvation of the sense of human dignity—the only trace of the highest truth or divine nature that we are able to recognize in ourselves and define."[31]

If we also assume that Herbert subscribes to Elzenberg's assertion that "Ethics teaches how to face existence with fortitude,"[32] we cannot help recalling that the Latin *virtus* can be translated as "virtue" but also as "stalwartness," "manliness," or "fortitude." It is not the manliness of the so-called real men or athletes of power, but, rather the manliness of the individual who is fully aware that there is no external authority that can make decisions for him, and who possesses a tragic (though not pessimistic)[33] consciousness of the unattainability of ideal harmony, perfection, or peace. What seems to be a superior value in this poetry is perpetual striving—in the spirit of the final "Be Faithful Go" from "The Envoy of Mr. Cogito"—rather than the attainment of any goal.[34] It is worth noting Herbert's frequent statements rejecting "calm," "certainty," or harmony considered as ultimate rewards: "I will not return to the source of calm" ("The Last Will," SS 47);

> only we shall meet a horrible fate
> flame and lamentation
> because baptized by the earth
> we were too dauntless in our certainty   ("Baptism," H 8)
>
> he would like to remain faithful
> to uncertain clarity
> ("Mr. Cogito and the Imagination," R 24, CR 19)

The aesthetic consequences of Herbert's ethical stance seem to be at variance with what I said a moment ago. It is undoubtedly true that, as one critic put it, "Herbert is one of those very few poets who make a Platonic association between Beauty (Art) and the Good."[35] But harmony is not a moral criterion for him, and perfection in an ethical sense is unattainable: how can these two convictions be reconciled with aesthetic perfection and harmony, without which great art is unimaginable? Herbert's solution to this problem is, once again, paradoxical. In his view, if we are to consider "taste" the aesthetic equivalent of conscience (as convincingly suggested in his poem "The Power of Taste"), it can be an ultimate criterion only insofar as it fixes a certain ideal point of orientation, which should be striven for but cannot possibly be reached. Sometimes, in certain epochs and countries, it cannot be reached simply because scrupulously to fulfill the dictates of taste in real life would result in a fall of the body's "precious capital—the head." But it is also impossible for more profound philosophical reasons, because "The most beautiful is the object / which does not exist" (SP 54, M 104): the attainment of ultimate aesthetic perfection would mean a severance of ties with the real world, a dissolution in nothingness.

An analogous argument is presented in reverse by an earlier poem "Five Men" (H 76–78, M 58–60). This is a story of five men condemned to death who, during the night before the execution, do not talk about important and weighty matters as one might expect, but about the most trivial details of everyday life. The poem's speaker—the poet himself—while meditating on the moment of death and its "garish light of obviousness," first asks himself: "so why have I been writing / unimportant poems on flowers." However, when he realizes what the condemned men have been talking about, he reaches an unexpected conclusion:

> thus one can use in poetry
> names of Greek shepherds
> one can attempt to catch the colour of morning sky
> write of love
> and also
> once again
> in dead earnest
> offer to the betrayed world
> a rose

The conclusion is unexpected, but nonetheless logical. The conjunction "thus"[36] plays exactly the same role here as "And nonetheless" in the poem "Priest," although the former's logical model of consecution seems to have nothing in common with the logical contradiction of the latter. The point in both cases is, however, the same: just as prayer is still possible despite the death of gods, so the nothingness of death does not preclude the need for art. Just as prayer will not reach any god, so poetry will not save the world— nevertheless, by speaking of the world, by offering it "in dead earnest . . . a rose," poetry at least expresses its own sense of "fidelity."

But what kind of art and poetry must this be? It cannot be the art of the "ornament-makers," the hired whitewashers of reality, those artists in a luxurious hell who are provided by Beelzebub "with calm, good board, and absolute isolation from hellish life" (P 74, C 61). At the same time, it cannot be the art of rhetorical didacticism that reflects the artist's conviction of his own moral superiority.[37] Neither can it be the relativistic and morally indifferent art that practices the principle of absolute liberty, resulting from

> the discovery
> that in the contemporary world
> there are no direct results
> no tyranny of sequence
> dictatorship of causality
> all thoughts
> actions
> objects
> phenomena
> lie side by side   (P 62, C 54)

And it cannot be hysterically expressionist art, the art of "a small broken soul / with a great self-pity" (N 52, M 138). Finally, it cannot be the art as it is conceived by a soulless "classic," who "never will . . . guess that the marble veins in the Baths of Diocletian are the blood vessels of slaves which have burst in the quarries" (H 145, C 8). What seems closest to Herbert's views is the conception of art presented in "Three Studies on the Subject of Realism"—an art that strives for perfection in revealing the world's conflicts but never attains its ultimate goal: it cannot be perfect, because, while forcing man to ponder moral alternatives, it also "imperceptibly give[s] a nudge to the balance" to help him decide.

IN CONCLUSION, I shall return to the problem of the moral message in Herbert's poetry, in order to supplement it with something as vital as it is underrated in most critical analyses of his work. I have mentioned more than once that the ethics of the author of *Pan Cogito* have no unequivocal and reliable support from any external authority. In this poetry man has to decide for himself; the transcendence of myth, art, philosophy, or religion may help him but cannot provide any unequivocal set of instructions. Another way to describe this problem is to reiterate that the implied author of Herbert's poetry, while longing for the heritage of old, traditional values, is soberly aware that those values have been lost; in today's world one can only try to revive them, but with uncertain results, or rather at the risk of near certain defeat. For Mr. Cogito there is no return to Arcadia.

However—and this seems to be the aspect of Herbert's poetry that is not sufficiently noticed and appreciated—it is even more out of the question that Mr. Cogito would agree to settle on the island of Utopia.[38] Just as he does not accept a conservative or regressive vision, he is also unable to accept the easy and illusory relief seemingly provided by visions projected into the future, utopias of perfection and harmony, according to which

> paradise will be at hand
> when the class struggle ends
> and when we start obtaining
> such and such amounts per acre   ("Vita," H 83)

In other words, just as in Herbert's poetry faithfulness or fidelity must do without any external authority, so does hope appear as *hope without guarantee*—no philosophy, no ideology, no vision of social system will assure us paradise on earth.[39] Mr. Cogito "accepts an inferior role / he won't inhabit history" ("Mr. Cogito's Game," P 73, C 60). His hope is calculated on a different scale:

> We are standing under the wall. Our youth has been
> taken off like a shirt from the condemned men. We
> wait. Before the fat bullet will sit down on the nape of
> the neck, ten, twenty years pass. The wall is high and
> strong. Behind the wall is a tree and a star. The tree
> pries at the wall with its roots. The star nibbles the
> stone like a mouse. In a hundred, two hundred years
> there will already be a small window.
> ("The Wall," H 130, C 29)

Is this "wall" around the isle of Utopia? "I don't like utopias," confessed the poet in a recent interview, "because they start with someone inventing an island and a marvelous social system but they end with concentration camps."[40] We should recall that, walls or no walls, it was usually hard for the happy inhabitants of the island of Utopia or the City of the Sun to leave. In Thomas More, one is struck by the passports and permits that were obligatory even for traveling about the island itself: a traveler caught without a passport outside his own district was to be punished as a deserter, and for a second offense the punishment was slavery.[41] It was perhaps in reference to this rule that another contemporary Polish author, Wisława Szymborska, who is in many respects close to Herbert, wrote a poem describing the island of Utopia—unmarred happiness, harmony, certainty, and perfection would reign there, were it not for one shortcoming: the island has no inhabitants. True, countless footprints can be seen on the sand—all of them, however, lead toward the sea.[42]

This is also the case with Herbert's hero, Mr. Cogito, who in recent years, while remaining an individualist and outsider, has quite unexpectedly become a model for the spiritual situation of contemporary Poles. Although defense seems hopeless, Mr. Cogito does not wish to leave the besieged City. But when anyone tries to make him happy by forcing him to remain permanently on an ideal island, Mr. Cogito refuses. In his choice to remain faithful to the human condition—suspended between frailty and perfection, experience and myth, disinheritance and heritage—he becomes not only an exile from Arcadia; he is also a fugitive from Utopia.

Notes

Introduction

1. I have in mind chiefly, among Polish critics, Jan Błoński, "Tradycja, ironia i głębsze znaczenie," *Poezja* (Warsaw), 3 (1970); Jerzy Kwiatkowski, "Klerk mężny," *Życie Literackie* (Cracow), 40 (1957), and "Imiona prostoty," in Kwiatkowski, *Klucze do wyobraźni* (Warsaw, 1964); Jan Józef Lipski, "Między historią i Arkadią wyobraźni," *Twórczość* (Warsaw), 1 (1962); Adam Michnik, "Glosa do rozmowy," *Krytyka* (Warsaw-London), 8 (1981), and "Potęga smaku," in Michnik, *Z dziejów honoru w Polsce* (Paris, 1985); Ryszard Przybylski, "Między cierpieniem a formą," in Przybylski, *To jest klasycyzm* (Warsaw, 1978); and Janusz Sławiński, "Tren Fortynbrasa," *Miesięcznik Literacki* (Warsaw), 1 (1967). I am particularly indebted to Błoński, Michnik, and Sławiński. As far as Western critics are concerned, I have in mind, above all, Alfred Alvarez, "Introduction to the Poetry of Zbigniew Herbert," in Herbert, *Selected Poems* (Penguin Books, 1968); Karl Dedecius, in particular "Anbau der Philosophie: Zbigniew Herbert auf der Suche nach Selbstgewissheit," in Dedecius, *Polnische Profile* (Frankfurt am Main, 1975); and numerous articles of Bogdana and John Carpenter, some of which will be referred to later. Only after having completed a draft of the Polish version of this book did I have the opportunity to read Andrzej Kaliszewski's study, *Gry Pana Cogito* (Cracow, 1982), the first book-length monograph on Herbert's poetry. Despite its many cogent analyses and observations, Kaliszewski's book is, unfortunately, not satisfactory as an attempt to grasp the essence of Herbert's poetic work as a whole.

2. Thus far, four books by Herbert have appeared in English translation: *Selected Poems*, trans. Czeslaw Milosz and Peter Dale Scott (Harmondsworth: Penguin Books, 1968); *Selected Poems* (a different selection), trans. John Carpenter and Bogdana Carpenter (Oxford: Oxford University Press, 1977); *Report from the Besieged City and Other Poems*, trans. John

Carpenter and Bogdana Carpenter (New York: Ecco Press, 1985); *Barbarian in the Garden* (essays), trans. Michael March and Jaroslaw Anders (Manchester: Carcanet, 1985).

3. Cf. the most characteristic and/or influential interpretations of this kind: Jarosław Marek Rymkiewicz, "Poeta i barbarzyńcy," in *Osnowa* (Lodz, 1964), rpt. in Rymkiewicz, *Czym jest klasycyzm?* (Warsaw, 1967); Przybylski, "Krzyk Marsjasza: O poezji Zbigniewa Herberta," *Współczesność* (Warsaw), 20 (1964); Julian Kornhauser, "Herbert: Z odległej prowincji," *Nowy Wyraz* (Warsaw), 1/2 (1973), rpt. in Kornhauser and Adam Zagajewski, *Świat nie przedstawiony* (Cracow, 1974); Artur Sandauer, "Głos, dzielony na czworo," *Kultura* (Warsaw), 7–9 (1976), and "Ewolucja polskiej poezji 1945–1968," *Polityka* (Warsaw), 18–20 (1979), both rpt. in Sandauer, *Zebrane pisma krytyczne,* vol. 1 (Warsaw, 1981).

4. The basic biographical data, although not free from euphemisms and omissions, are included in Jadwiga Bandrowska-Wróblewska, "Nota biograficzna," in Herbert, *Poezje wybrane* (Warsaw, 1973). Some interesting details are added by Dedecius's brief essay "Zbigniew Herbert," in Dedecius, *Überall ist Polen* (Frankfurt am Main, 1974), and the interview-article by W. L. Webb, "Exemplary Poet in a Traumatic World," *Guardian* (August 2, 1981). Two extensive interviews published in Polish underground periodicals deserve to be mentioned here as extremely valuable addenda—practically the only ones of this kind in the Polish press—in which Herbert expresses overt opinions on his own biography, convictions, the autobiographical background of some of his poems, etc.: "Płynie się zawsze do źródeł pod prąd, z prądem płyną śmiecie: Rozmowa ze Zbigniewem Herbertem," interv. Adam Michnik, *Krytyka* (Warsaw-London), 8 (1981); "Wypluć z siebie wszystko: Rozmowa ze Zbigniewem Herbertem," interv. Jacek Trznadel, *Kultura Niezależna* (Warsaw), 14 (1985).

5. "Płynie się," 59; cf. Dedecius, "Zbigniew Herbert," 62.

6. In the case of the poem "September 17" (first published in the Paris monthly *Kultura,* 5 [1982]), the historical background is twofold—the poem refers to the Soviet invasion of 1939, and it was written during the period of Solidarity, when Poland was threatened by yet another invasion from the East.

7. Webb, "Exemplary Poet."

8. Elzenberg's influence on the shaping of Herbert's outlook is presented in a detailed annd knowledgeable way by Dedecius, "In der Höhle der Philosophen: Über Zbigniew Herbert," *Deutsche Studien,* 47 (1974), rpt. with two other essays in Dedecius, "Anbau der Philosophie." This article, incidentally, offers the most insightful analysis of Herbert's philosophical problematics to date.

9. On Herbert's complicated relationship with *Tygodnik Powszechny* see his own confessions in "Płynie się," 61–62.

10. The atmosphere of this event is well rendered in the diary by Leopold Tyrmand, *Dziennik 1954* (London, 1980), 71–73.

11. "Płynie się," 52. All translations of quotations in this book are mine, unless otherwise stated.

12. Tyrmand, *Dziennik*, 32–33, 80–81, 168.

13. For details see the interview "Jeśli masz dwie drogi . . . Rozmowa ze Zbigniewem Herbertem," interv. Krystyna Nastulanka, *Polityka* (Warsaw), 9 (1972), rpt. in Nastulanka, *Sami o sobie: Rozmowy z pisarzami i uczonymi* (Warsaw, 1975).

14. On Herbert's stay in the United States see the interview "Zbigniew Herbert w Ameryce," *Ameryka* (Warsaw), 168 (1973). Interesting observations on the mark that the American experience has left in the poet's work can be found in Bogdana and John Carpenter, "The Recent Poetry of Zbigniew Herbert," *World Literature Today*, 51 (1977), 212.

15. This was the famous "Letter of the 59." A reprint can be found in *Aneks* (London), 11 (1976), 12–14.

1. Antinomies

1. The notion of "the implied author," as parallel to Wolfgang Iser's "implied reader," seems to me the closest equivalent of what was known in Russian Formalist theory as "obraz avtora" and is usually rendered in Polish literary theory as "autor wewnętrzny." In this sense, "the implied author" is "the projection of a creative personality" implied within the structure of a literary work, which cannot be identified with either the real author or the narrator/speaker. Cf. Edward Balcerzan, *Styl i poetyka twórczości dwujęzycznej Brunona Jasieńskiego* (Wroclaw, 1968), 19–26. See also, for more elaborate classifications, Janusz Sławiński, "O kategorii podmiotu lirycznego," in *Wiersz i poezja*, ed. Jan Trzynadlowski (Wroclaw, 1966); Aleksandra Okopień-Sławińska, "Relacje osobowe w literackiej komunikacji," in *Problemy socjologii literatury*, ed. Janusz Sławiński (Wroclaw, 1971).

2. "Spór o nową sztukę," *Nowy Wyraz* (Warsaw), 1/2 (1973), 10.

3. For an insightful comment on this see Jan Józef Lipski, "Między historią i Arkadią wyobraźni," *Twórczość* (Warsaw), 1 (1962).

4. For details, see any biography of Wyspiański; for example, Wojciech Natanson, *Stanisław Wyspiański: Próba nowego spojrzenia* (Poznan, 1969), 203–204; Alicja Okońska, *Stanisław Wyspiański* (Warsaw, 1971), 362. The Wyspiański issue in connection with Herbert's "Wawel" was first illuminated by Kazimierz Wyka, "Składniki świetlnej struny," *Życie Literackie* (Cracow), 42 (1956), rpt. in Wyka, *Rzecz wyobraźni* (Warsaw, 1959), 247.

5. My discussion here is basically in accord with Wyka's interpretation of the poem.

6. Cf. Herbert's characteristic confession in one of his essays, written after he had visited the cave paintings in Lascaux: "Never before had I felt a stronger or more reassuring conviction: I am a citizen of the earth, an inheritor not only of the Greeks and Romans but of almost the whole of infinity." *Barbarian in the Garden,* trans. Michael March and Jaroslaw Anders (Manchester: Carcanet, 1985), 16.

7. The word "disinheritance" (*wydziedziczenie*) is used, although with a narrower meaning, by Artur Sandauer in "Głos, dzielony na czworo," in Sandauer, *Zebrane pisma krytyczne,* vol. 1, (Warsaw, 1981), 439.

8. "A sense of bereavement, a multi-level orphanhood, so to speak, is a recurrent theme in Herbert's work," wrote Andrzej Kijowski in "Outcast of Obvious Forms," *Polish Perspectives* (Warsaw), 2 (1966), 35–36 (trans. by *Polish Perspectives*).

9. Cf., for example, the characteristic title of an early review by Marek Skwarnicki, "Wygnany arkadyjczyk" [An Exiled Arcadian], *Tygodnik Powszechny* (Cracow), 44 (1957).

10. Herbert's geographic and cultural dualism strongly resembles the concept of intersecting axes sketched by Czeslaw Milosz in *The Witness of Poetry* (Cambridge, Mass.: Harvard University Press, 1983), ch. 1.

11. Sandauer, "Głos," 439–440.

12. This motif was brought to light by Kijowski in his review of *Barbarzyńca w ogrodzie,* "Pielgrzym," *Twórczość* (Warsaw), 5 (1963), rpt. in Kijowski, *Arcydzieło nieznane* (Cracow, 1964).

13. Cf. the numerous interpretations of this poem, particularly in Jan Błoński, "Tradycja, ironia i głębsze znaczenie," *Poezja* (Warsaw), 3 (1970); Sandauer, "Głos"; Andrzej Kaliszewski, *Gry Pana Cogito* (Cracow, 1982).

14. Herbert has analyzed this "feeling of guilt in the face of masterpieces" from another, psychological angle in "Akropol i duszyczka," *Więź* (Warsaw), 4 (1973).

15. All italics in quotations are mine, unless otherwise stated.

16. Its meaning was explained in this way in Kijowski, "Róża i las. O twórczości Zbigniewa Herberta," *Radar* (Warsaw) 12, (1965).

17. "The dream will be interrupted by the sudden entrance / of three tall men made of rubber and iron / they will check the name they will check the fear . . ."

18. Also in his essays. Even if we overlook the ones that reflect on the underside of mythologized history—such as "Sprawa Samos," *Odra* (Wroclaw), 3 (1972), which describes the Greece of Pericles as it was in historical reality—the essay "Próba opisania krajobrazu greckiego," *Poezja* (Warsaw), 9 (1966), in which even the Mediterranean landscape seems to the narrator to have been permeated by "brute force and violence," is a striking example of that attitude.

19. Cf. remarks of Ireneusz Krzemiński, "Zbigniew Herbert i tradycja," *Współczesność* (Warsaw), 25 (1971).

20. Henryk Krzeczkowski, "Przymierzanie się do historii," *Tygodnik Powszechny* (Cracow), 6 (1972).

21. Cf. Herbert's remarks on "the two catastrophes"—that of war and that of the postwar times—in his interview "Płynie się zawsze do źródeł pod prąd, z prądem płyną śmiecie. Rozmowa ze Zbigniewem Herbertem," interv. Adam Michnik, *Krytyka* (Warsaw-London), 8 (1981), 50n.

22. In spite of this obviousness, there is no lack of tendentious critical interpretations, which consider, for instance, the bitter prose poem "Attempt to Dissolve Mythology" (C 17) as "an attempt to leave the circle of mythology, . . . the mythology of war and occupation, the excess of which is clearly a burden to the poet." Jan Witan, "Poezji wiedza kojąca," *Poezja* (Warsaw), 4 (1970), 83.

23. On this subject see, among others, W. W. Douglas, "The Meanings of 'Myth' in Modern Criticism," *Modern Philology*, 1 (1952–53); *Myth: A Symposium*, ed. Thomas A. Sebeok (Bloomington, Ind., 1958); Geoffrey S. Kirk, *Myth: Its Meaning and Functions in Ancient and Other Cultures* (Berkeley, 1970); K. K. Ruthven, *Myth* (London, 1976).

24. The presence of this comprehension, which forms, as it were, the second semantic level above the primary meaning of a sign, is particularly crucial. Cf. Roland Barthes's conception in *Mythologies*, trans. Annette Lavers (London, 1972).

25. Leslie A. Fiedler, "Archetype and Signature: A Study of the Relationship between Biography and Poetry," *Sewanee Review*, 10 (1952). On the relationship between myth and literature, see, among others, Maud Bodkin, *Archetypal Patterns in Poetry* (London, 1934); Northrop Frye, *Anatomy of Criticism* (Princeton, 1957); John Holloway, "The Concept of Myth in Literature," in *Metaphor and Symbol*, ed. L. C. Knights and Basil Cottle (London, 1960); *Myth and Literature: Contemporary Theory and Practice*, ed. John B. Vickery (Lincoln, Neb., 1966); William Righter, *Myth and Literature* (London, 1975).

26. T. S. Eliot, "*Ulysses*, Order and Myth," in *The Modern Tradition: Backgrounds of Modern Literature*, ed. Richard Ellmann and Charles T. Feidelson (New York, 1965).

27. Cf. several different interpretations of this poem: Jacek Łukasiewicz, "Studium przedmiotu," in Łukasiewicz, *Szmaciarze i bohaterowie* (Cracow, 1962); Jarosław Marek Rymkiewicz, "Krzesło," *Twórczość* (Warsaw), 1 (1970); Debra Nicholson Częstochowski, "Herbert's 'Study of the Object': A Reading," *Polish Review* (New York), 4 (1975).

28. This fact has been emphasized particularly by Błoński, "Tradycja, ironia."

29. Cf. the extensive interpretation of Herbert's poem "Pan Cogito obserwuje w lustrze swoją twarz" in Per-Arne Bodin, "The Barbarian and the Mirror: An Analysis of One Poem in Zbigniew Herbert's Poetical Cycle 'Pan Cogito'," *Scando-Slavica* (Copenhagen), 27 (1981).

30. The predominance of "whiteness" in Herbert's poetry has been

pointed out by Alicja Lisiecka, "Wiersze zebrane Herberta," in Lisiecka, *Przewodnik po literaturze krajowej* (London, 1975), 51–52. Krzysztof Dybciak, "W poszukiwaniu istoty i utraconych wartości," in Dybciak, *Gry i katastrofy* (Warsaw, 1980), emphasizes the significance of "grayness" and makes this observation the starting point for an insightful analysis of Herbert's ethics and aesthetics.

31. Herbert points out in one of his essays that "A Doric temple should display bright reds, blues and ochre. The most ruthless restorer would wince at such an ordeal. We wish to see the Greeks washed by the rains, drenched white, devoid of passion and cruelty." *Barbarian*, 28.

32. Cf. remarks of Kaliszewski, *Gry*, 94.

33. The role of the motifs of "light" and "darkness," in connection with that of "earth," has been extensively analyzed by Jolanta Dudek, "Zatopiony w ciemnych promieniach ziemi . . . (O poezji Zbigniewa Herberta)," *Ruch Literacki* (Cracow), 5 (1971).

34. Likewise in his essays. Cf. his characteristic reflections on the light in the paintings of Piero della Francesca, *Barbarian*, 148–162.

35. Cf. observations of Dudek, "Zatopiony," 293–295.

36. Cf. a thorough interpretation by Wiesław Paweł Szymański, "Zbigniew Herbert, 'Ścieżka'," in Szymański, *Outsiderzy i słowiarze* (Wroclaw, 1973).

37. The role of this particular opposition has been emphasized by the critics from the very beginning of Herbert's career. Cf., among others, Zdzisław Najder, "O poezji Zbigniewa Herberta," *Twórczość* (Warsaw), 9 (1956); Jerzy Kwiatkowski, "Klerk mężny," *Życie Literackie* (Cracow), 40 (1957). Cf. also the broad treatment of this problem by Kaliszewski, *Gry*, in his chapter "Między konkretem i abstrakcją (inne)."

38. Wyka, in his early review, had written about Herbert's taking the side "of the concrete against the abstract." Wyka, "Składniki," 244. Likewise, Zbigniew Bieńkowski later interpreted Herbert's work as "a poetry of the concrete struggling against the abstract": "W obronie gliny ludzkiej," *Nowe Książki* (Warsaw), 5 (1972). Bieńkowski's review, incidentally, is an interesting example of an exaggerated reverse reaction to the popular labeling of Herbert as a "Classicist." Although he is basically correct in his reading of Herbert's poetry as a "defense of the individual against history's usurpation," Bieńkowski goes so far as to interpret, for example, the poem "The Substance" as an unequivocal vindication of the antiheroic "living plasma" of society; this, as I shall demonstrate later, is an incomplete and misleading conception.

39. This particular motif is considered to be the key to Herbert's poetry by Anna Kamieńska, "Niewierny Tomasz i świat," *Twórczość* (Warsaw), 10/11 (1957). Cf. Marian Pankowski, "Krajowe nowości poetyckie," *Kultura* (Paris), 12 (1956), 146.

40. The paradoxical character of this problem increases as we move the

opposition of the abstract versus the concrete from the cognitive to the political and moral levels. The unconsidered acceptance of the thesis that Herbert is a programmatic defender of the concrete caused Wyka, for example, to read "Elegy of Fortinbras" in a dangerously oversimplified way, as praise for political pragmatism. Wyka, "Tren Fortynbrasa," *Literatura* (Warsaw), 7 (1972), rpt. in Wyka, *Rzecz wyobraźni,* 2nd enlarged ed. (Warsaw, 1977). Kaliszewski (*Gry,* 184) is right to maintain that the fact of Fortinbras's being "possessed by the pathological cult of the concrete" does not necessarily mean the author's approval of this character. Yet Stanisław Dąbrowski was no less correct in his earlier, very penetrating observation that the supposed pragmatism of Fortinbras is, in fact, his own self-delusion: "Contrary to unimportant appearances, abstract ideas are the lot of Fortinbras, because the opposition between the ruling power and the ruled one is an opposition between the schematic and the concrete, between the intent and existence, between the projected plan and *life.*" Dąbrowski, "Hamlet i Fortynbras," *Tygodnik Powszechny* (Cracow), 8 (1971); italics are the author's.

41. The parallel with Białoszewski was suggested in particular by Sandauer, "Głos"; that with Ponge by Kwiatkowski, "Imiona prostoty," in Kwiatkowski, *Klucze do wyobraźni* (Warsaw, 1964), and by Jacek Trznadel, "Przykład Ponge'a," in Trznadel, *Płomień obdarzony rozumem* (Warsaw, 1978). The latter analogy has been examined thoroughly by Kaliszewski, *Gry,* 214n.

42. On this subject, see a direct comment by the poet himself: "I experienced, if not personally, then certainly as a witness, quite a number of shameful collapses [*niejedną kompromitację*] of ideologies, breakdowns of artificially created images of reality, capitulations of faith to the facts. And then the realm of things, the realm of nature seemed to me a foothold, and also a point of departure leading to the creation of an image of the world that would correspond to our experience. After the false prophets left, things, so to speak, revealed their innocent faces, unblemished by the lies." "Rozmowa o pisaniu wierszy," in Herbert, *Poezje wybrane* (Warsaw, 1973), 15–16.

43. It is significant that the stool is the addressee of the poem. This kind of dialogical approach to an object will vanish in "Pebble" or "Wooden Die."

44. This problem, considered as Herbert's assault against transcendence, has been closely examined by Bogdana and John Carpenter, particularly in "Zbigniew Herbert and the Imperfect Poem," *Malahat Review* (Victoria, B.C.), 54 (1980).

45. In this sense, a number of other poems suggest that, just as "white" and "black" are paradoxically close to each other, the distance from divine to satanic perfection is not far. Cf. the interpretation of the Faustian ending of the poem "Path" in Szymański, "Zbigniew Herbert," 350: "the realiza-

tion of a *full,* perfect man is possible only with the help of an irrational *negative* force" (Szymański's italics).

46. Jan Prokop, "Rozmowy z Cezarem," *Więź* (Warsaw), 3 (1962), 150.

47. Cf. Janusz Maciejewski, "Poeta dnia dzisiejszego," *Tygodnik Kulturalny* (Warsaw), 19 (1972): "Perfection, order, harmony are notions that seem to Herbert not only alien, but hostile. For they are devoid of human concreteness. Frailty and weakness are what is human and earthly." Here we encounter yet another oversimplification. Using as his chief evidence the same misinterpreted poem, "The Substance," Maciejewski (like Bieńkowski, whom I have already quoted) overlooks the fact that dogmatic perfection imposed from above on the one hand and individual, spontaneous striving for perfection on the other are two different things for Herbert.

48. On the aesthetic plane, an analogous meaning seems to be contained in the ending of "Study of the Object," where a perfect rendition of the object by the artist is identified with "reveal[ing] . . . the pupil of death."

59. Cf. the succinct and pertinent conclusion of an essay by Madeline G. Levine, "Zbigniew Herbert: In Defense of Civilization," in Levine, *Contemporary Polish Poetry 1925–1975* (Twayne Publishers: Boston, 1981), 136: "Zbigniew Herbert is a poet-moralist whose insistence on moral perfection coexists with an unblinking acceptance of human imperfection."

50. "Ozdobne a prawdziwe" (N 34). Incidentally, in translating this title as "Ornamental yet True," B. and J. Carpenter committed, in my view, a minor but significant error of interpretation. The ambiguous Polish conjunction "a" should be translated, in the context of this particular poem, as "Ornamental *and* True," or even "Ornamental *versus* True."

51. This was the way the majority of critics who dealt with this poem read it. Cf., in particular, Kwiatkowski, "Klerk."

52. Cf., for instance, Reuel K. Wilson, "Three Contemporary Slavic Poets: A View from the Other Side," *New Quarterly Cave* (Hamilton, New Zealand), 4 (1976), 51–52. Kaliszewski (*Gry,* 201) is clearly wrong when he identifies this third kind of realism with "the Socialist Realist pictorial arts, and then with the same kind of literature, in its more insane manifestations," assuming that Herbert "decided . . . to ridicule—in a general way—all extremes." In fact, in none of the three parts of the poem do we hear a tone of ridicule or mockery; the reader would have to be very self-assured to identify what is described in the poem's third part as "a nudge to the balance" with the "extremes" and "insane manifestations" of Socialist Realism. A secondary argument—the sentence in the poem about "canvases divided into the right side and the left side" corresponds interestingly with an early poem by Herbert, "Fra Angelico: Męczeństwo świętych Kosmy i Damiana," *Tygodnik Powszechny* (Cracow), 19 (1951), which consists of a description of "The Left Side of the Painting," "The

Right Side of the Painting" and "The Background." Fra Angelico would hardly qualify as a Socialist Realist.

53. On this subject, see also the extensive discussion in Kaliszewski, *Gry,* the chapters "Bogowie i ludzie" and "Remont w zaświatach."

54. In speaking of angels in Herbert's poems, Kaliszewski introduces a pertinent distinction between the "folklore" angel and the angel as portrayed in the official or dogmatic Christian iconography (*Gry,* 115).

55. Ibid., 136.

56. Cf. the comprehensive interpretation in Łukasiewicz, "Przesłuchanie anioła," in Łukasiewicz, *Zagłoba w piekle* (Cracow, 1965).

57. An interpretive suggestion of Łukasiewicz, ibid., 173–174.

58. Cf. Kwiatkowski's interpretation in "Herbert niezawodny," in Kwiatkowski, *Notatki o poezji i krytyce* (Cracow, 1975), 126–127.

59. For analyses of some of these poems, see Ryszard Przybylski, "Między cierpieniem a formą," in Przybylski, *To jest klasycyzm* (Warsaw, 1978), 132–145, and Kaliszewski, *Gry,* 95–98.

60. The poem was first published in *Tygodnik Powszechny* (Cracow), 40 (1951).

61. The interpretations were influenced principally by Przybylski's essay "Krzyk Marsjasza," *Współczesność* (Warsaw), 20 (1964).

62. For a more extensive discussion of "Fragment," see Konrad W. Tatarowski, "Od 'stylu-monologu' do 'stylu-dialogu'. Uwagi o poezji Zbigniewa Herberta," *Zeszyty Naukowe Uniwersytetu Łódzkiego, Nauki Humanistyczno-Społeczne* (Lodz), I, 50 (1979), 62n.

63. For a concise presentation of the controversy, see, among others, Ruthven, *Myth,* 53–55, and Lillian Feder, *Ancient Myth in Modern Poetry* (Princeton, 1971), 34–59 .

64. Cf. the comment of Adam Michnik, "Glosa do rozmowy," *Krytyka* (Warsaw-London), 8 (1981), 67.

65. Marta Wyka, "Jak oswajać konieczność, czyli o twórczości Herberta," *Dialog* (Warsaw), 7 (1971), 100.

2. Metaphors

1. See the lucid presentation in Wayne C. Booth, *A Rhetoric of Irony* (Chicago, 1974), 21–24.

2. "Irony," in *Princeton Encyclopedia of Poetry and Poetics,* ed. A. Preminger (Princeton, 1974), 407.

3. Cleanth Brooks, "Irony as a Principle of Structure," in *Literary Opinion in America,* ed. M. D. Zabel (New York, 1951). See also Brooks, *The Well-Wrought Urn* (London, 1949).

4. Andrzej Kaliszewski criticizes this state of affairs in *Gry Pana Cogito* (Cracow, 1982), 81; he himself, however, with the exception of a few

analyses of verse structure, goes no further than a vague statement on Herbert's "Classical diction."

5. The observations of Jan Błoński, "Tradycja, ironia i głębsze znaczenie," *Poezja* (Warsaw), 3 (1970), Jerzy Kwiatkowski, "Imiona prostoty," in Kwiatkowski, *Klucze do wyobraźni* (Warsaw, 1964), and Konrad W. Tatarowski, "Od 'stylu-monologu' do 'stylu-dialogu'. Uwagi o poezji Zbigniewa Herberta," *Zeszyty Naukowe Uniwersytetu Łódzkiego, Nauki Humanistyczno-Społeczne* (Lodz), I, 50 (1979), are particularly valuable. Jan Pieszczachowicz, "Stąd do nicości," *Współczesność* (Warsaw), 14 (1970), has made a few relevant, if superficial, remarks on Herbert's vision of language as "A hell of conventionality." Jan Prokop, "Epitafium dla duszyczki," in Prokop, *Lekcja rzeczy* (Cracow, 1972), is the author of a number of interesting observations on the "conversational" character of Herbert's poetry, or, more precisely, its being rooted in "the colloquial language of the intellectual elite." This kind of sociolinguistic approach deserves a more extensive elaboration; I refer to it at times in speaking of the workings of irony in Herbert.

6. What is particularly striking is the fiasco of strictly linguistic approaches. I have in mind two articles by Ewa Ostrowska, "Wiersz Zbigniewa Herberta 'O róży," *Język Polski* (Cracow), 2/3 (1973), and "Składnia i kompozycja w wierszu dzisiejszym. (Na podstawie wierszy Zbigniewa Herberta, Tymoteusza Karpowicza, Tadeusza Mocarskiego)," *Ruch Literacki* (Cracow), 2 (1974).

7. Janusz Maciejewski, "Poeta dnia dzisiejszego," *Tygodnik Kulturalny* (Warsaw), 19 (1972), writes about "a certain indifference in Herbert toward matters of 'craftsmanship'." Jacek Trznadel, "Kamienowanie mądrości," in Trznadel, *Płomień obdarzony rozumem* (Warsaw, 1978), 134, goes even further: "In Herbert's poetry, beams pass through the word and stop on situations and holy books."

8. An expression used by Herbert in a debate "Spór o nową sztukę," *Nowy Wyraz* (Warsaw), 1/2 (1973). The same speech by Herbert was reprinted in an enlarged version in "Poeta wobec współczesności," *Odra* (Wroclaw), 11 (1972), 49–50.

9. "Rozmowa o pisaniu wierszy," in Herbert, *Poezje wybrane* (Warsaw, 1973), 13, 16. "A quotation from another great poet" is a distych from "Child of Europe" by Czeslaw Milosz, characteristically modified by Herbert. Herbert's poem "To Ryszard Krynicki—A Letter" (R 26, CR 21), which contains polemical references to the conception of language advanced by the younger "generation of 1968," offers an even more important programmatic declaration on language.

10. Kwiatkowski, "Klerk mężny," *Życie Literackie* (Cracow), 40 (1957).

11. This is confirmed, incidentally, by Herbert's critical articles and reviews, more than a dozen of which appeared in literary periodicals during the 1940s and 1950s. See, among others, his especially interesting re-

marks on metaphor, poetic semantics, and verse construction in "Uwagi o poezji Józefa Czechowicza," *Twórczość* (Warsaw), 9 (1955). Herbert's interest in matters of poetic technique—for all his barely masked dislike of the ideology of the analyzed poet—can be seen in his early essay on Mayakovsky, "Warsztat Majakowskiego," *Arkona* (Poznan-Bydgoszcz),10–12 (1948).

12. This fact has been perhaps underestimated by Błoński, who in his otherwise excellent essay ("Tradycja, ironia") states too categorically: "It is *exactly the convention* that in Herbert's view grasps *the truth of life* in the most perfect way" (27; Błoński's italics). This is both true and false; in the sphere of language as well as that of general aesthetics Herbert's attitude to the problem of convention is noticeably ambivalent. What is to be done, for example, with the poem "Chinese Wallpaper" (N 46), where the description of the title object—which symbolizes pure convention—ends with the following statement: "One cannot offend the world more than this"?

13. The frequent presence of "paradoxical formulas" in Herbert's work is mentioned by Marek Jodłowski, "Pan Cogito i anioł Ironii," *Opole* (Opole), 6 (1972). Jan Pieszczachowicz, "Pana Cogito drogi wolności," *Miesięcznik Literacki* (Warsaw), 8 (1974), has written, in discussing *Pan Cogito,* about Herbert's "paradoxical logic" and "poetics of paradox."

14. Adam Czerniawski, "Nowe wiersze Herberta," *Kultura* (Paris), 11 (1963), 140, interprets this as a consequence of Herbert's "basic paradoxical assumption that our 'normal' observations are thoroughly false." I would not agree, however, with Czerniawski's remark that such an assumption is marked by "the cold logic of the absurd."

15. In my linguistic perception, the Polish word *grzechotka* signifies primarily, if not solely, a *child's* toy rattle.

16. Another motivation for this image is the symbolic connection between "air" and "divinity," which I have already pointed out.

17. Kaliszewski, *Gry,* 145, points to the similarity between this poem and Andrzej Bursa's poem "Dno piekła" [Hell's Bottom]. It is unlikely that Herbert could have written his poem "later" than Bursa; Bursa's poem was written in 1957, while Herbert's book of poems had begun to be typeset by February 4, 1957 (*Hermes, pies i gwiazda,* 180).

18. The role of the point of view in Herbert's poetry has been the subject of many analyses; most of them, however, have dealt with this in a much more general sense than I do in this chapter. See, in particular, Błoński, "Tradycja, ironia."

19. Cf. remarks of Kaliszewski, *Gry,* 166–169.

20. Incidentally, the same image of ants hiding in a watch occurs, in even more expressive form, in another prose poem, "Wristwatch" (N 45, M 134).

21. This was not always true, though; Ryszard Przybylski, "Między

cierpieniem a formą," in Przybylski, *To jest klasycyzm* (Warsaw, 1978), 134–135, reminds us, for instance, of Raphael's fresco and of the Renaissance discussion of Marsyas's suffering.

22. The notion of apocrypha was first introduced into Herbert criticism most probably by Trznadel, "Herberta apokryf ironiczny," in Trznadel, *Płomień*. Kaliszewski, *Gry*, 96–97, proposes the germ "gloss" instead, which would have certain advantages. It is worth noting that the same "apocryphal" technique is also used by Herbert in his plays (*The Philosophers' Den, Reconstruction of the Poet*) and essays (for example, "Apokryfy holenderskie" [Dutch Apocrypha], *Twórczość* [Warsaw], 7 [1979]).

23. Przybylski, "Między cierpieniem," 141–142, interprets this poem as a polemical allusion to the painting "The Sacrifice of Iphigenia" by Timantes, and especially to Agamemnon's famous gesture of veiling his face. It does not seem, however, that this is exactly the poem's semantic center of gravity. Cf. also Kaliszewski, *Gry*, 100–101.

24. From the play *Reconstruction of the Poet*, in which a few of Herbert's poems are recited by Homer, who is the play's main character.

25. Incidentally, what we are dealing with here is the combination of a gaze focused upon a detail and a gaze reaching beneath the surface: the sight of the ear strikes the speaker so much because against the lamplight he is able to see it "with living blood / inside it."

26. More than one reviewer of *Hermes, pies i gwiazda* remarked upon the predominance of the parable over other genres in that volume; see, for example, J[ulian] P[rzyboś], "Nowy zbiór Zbigniewa Herberta," *Przegląd Kulturalny* (Warsaw), 42 (1957); sometimes, however, the term *bajki* (fables) was also employed. Leopold Tyrmand, *Dziennik 1954* (London, 1980), 168, mentions Herbert as writing "poems and fables" in 1954. What he means by fables is in all likelihood some of the prose poems that form the second part of *Hermes*. Among today's critics, Kaliszewski, *Gry*, 174n., analyzes in detail Herbert's methods of "demythologization of the structure of the fable." Wiesława Wantuch, "Tekst jako pretekst," *Nurt* (Poznan), 1 (1981), distinguishes the "fairy-tale (folk fable)," "children's story," and "school essay" as the three *einfache Formen* that Herbert refers to in his prose poems of that kind.

27. On the function of the child's point of view see remarks of Wantuch, "Tekst jako pretekst."

28. See, among others, D. C. Muecke, *The Compass of Irony* (London, 1969), 91; Muecke, *Irony* (London, 1970), 57n.

29. The same can be said about, for instance, "Railway Landscapes" (H 147), in which the childlike speaker scares himself, as it were, by construing metaphors such as "the round guillotine of minutes," "the black monster"; since we know that they are supposed to signify a railway-station and a locomotive, we cannot really take the speaker's fears at face value.

30. This was pointed out by Błoński, "Tradycja, ironia," 35.

3. Ironies

1. Instead, the reader may come across rather peculiar explanations, according to which irony would seem to be something of a cure for indigestion: "Moralization must be done with charm in order to be digestible. Therefore Herbert, as a moralist and philosopher, resorts to the weapons of irony, skepticism, and humor." Jan Zabieglik, "Poeta kultury," *Kierunki* (Warsaw), 12 (1974).

2. Jan Błoński, "Tradycja, ironia i głębsze znaczenie," *Poezja* (Warsaw), 3 (1970).

3. The fundamental works on this subject are: Søren Kierkegaard, *The Concept of Irony: With Constant Reference to Socrates,* trans. L. M. Capel (London, 1966); J. A. K. Thomson, *Irony: An Historical Introduction* (Cambridge, 1927); Rudolf Jancke, *Das Wesen der Ironie: Eine Strukturanalyse ihrer Erscheinungsformen* (Leipzig, 1929); G. G. Sedgewick, *Of Irony: Especially in Drama* (Toronto, 1935); Vladimir Jankélévitch, *L'ironie* (Paris, 1936); Alan Reynolds Thompson, *The Dry Mock: A Study of Irony in Drama* (Berkeley, 1948); Beda Allemann, *Ironie und Dichtung* (Pfullingen, 1956); Norman Knox, *The Word IRONY and its Context, 1500–1755* (Durham, 1961); Karlheinz Stäcker, *Ironie und Ironiker* (Mainz, 1963); S. J. E. Dikkers, *Ironie als vorm van communicatie* (The Hague, 1969); Ernst Behler, *Klassische Ironie, Romantische Ironie, Tragische Ironie: Zum Ursprung dieser Begriffe* (Darmstadt, 1972); D. C. Muecke, *The Compass of Irony* (London, 1969); Muecke, *Irony* (London, 1970); Wayne C. Booth, *A Rhetoric of Irony* (Chicago, 1974).

4. The distinction of Muecke, *Irony,* 49n, 63n.

5. Booth, *A Rhetoric,* 53.

6. Błoński, "Tradycja, ironia."

7. Cf., for example, Michał Głowiński, Aleksandra Okopień-Sławińska, Janusz Sławiński, *Zarys teorii literatury* (Warsaw, 1967), 293.

8. See Robert C. Elliot, *The Literary Persona* (Chicago, 1982), 19n.

9. I have in mind the narrower sense of the term "dramatic monologue," that is to say, the specific lyrical method of employing a dramatic speaker, rather than the genre in general.

10. Muecke, *The Compass,* 64n, 64, 87.

11. Ibid., 91; also Muecke, *Irony,* 59.

12. Muecke, *The Compass,* 92.

13. Cf. reflections on the role of irony in this poem in Jacek Łukasiewicz, *Laur i ciało* (Warsaw, 1971), 101–103.

14. A. Alvarez, "Introduction," in Zbigniew Herbert, *Selected Poems* (Harmondsworth: Penguin Books, 1968), 12.

15. Cf. particularly Booth, *A Rhetoric.* Dikkers, *Ironie,* suggests a division of roles into "the ironist," "the insider," and "the irony-deaf person."

16. On sarcasm as the most primitive form of so-called overt irony see Muecke, *The Compass*, 54.

17. Booth, *A Rhetoric*, 49n.

18. Ibid., 73.

19. Cf. the above-quoted opinions of Zbigniew Bieńkowski, "W obronie gliny ludzkiej," *Nowe Książki* (Warsaw), 5 (1972). Likewise, Janusz Maciejewski, "Poeta moralnej odpowiedzialności. (O poezji Zbigniewa Herberta)," in *Lektury i problemy* (Warsaw, 1976), 595n., maintains that the speaker's "solidarity with the characters" (those characters who "love life," as the context indicates) is a dominant tendency within the poem.

20. E.g., the many earlier poems that stemmed from the war experience and were concerned precisely with "the beautiful dead." Cf. also the specific problem of the tradition of Dutch culture and its attitude to heroism, which has drawn Herbert's attention in the past few years. I have in mind a few essays of his, such as "Temat niebohaterski," *Więź* (Warsaw), 11/12 (1979), "Apokryfy holenderskie," *Twórczość* (Warsaw), 7 (1979), and "Martwa natura z wędzidłem," *Twórczość*, 1 (1982), in which his ambiguous—half-sympathetic and half-critical—attitude toward the "sound republican spirit" of the Dutch finds expression ("Apokryfy," 11).

21. As far as I know, Adam Czerniawski, "Nowe wiersze Herberta," *Kultura* (Paris), 11 (1963), was the first critic to apply the term "dramatic monologue" to some of the poems from *Studium przedmiotu*.

22. Robert Langbaum, *The Poetry of Experience: The Dramatic Monologue in Modern Literary Tradition* (New York, 1963).

23. In particular, in Milosz's wartime sequence "Voices of Poor People." See also Milosz's remarks on the relationship between irony and the dramatic monologue in *Kontynenty* (Paris, 1958), 70–71; and *Prywatne obowiązki* (Paris, 1972), 41.

24. Jerzy Kwiatkowski, "Imiona prostoty," in Kwiatkowski, *Klucze do wyobraźni* (Warsaw, 1964), 363–364. This aspect is ignored in another interpretation of the poem: Maciejewski, "Zbigniew Herbert: 'U wrót doliny',"in *Czytamy wiersze*, 2nd ed. (Warsaw, 1973).

25. Janusz Sławiński, "Zbigniew Herbert, 'Tren Fortynbrasa'," in Teresa Kostkiewiczowa, Aleksandra Okopień-Sławińska, Janusz Sławiński, *Czytamy utwory współczesne: Analizy* (Warsaw, 1967).

26. Although he could not be accused of lack of erudition, Kazimierz Wyka once again fails as a Herbert critic in interpreting this poem. In "Tren Fortynbrasa," *Literatura* (Warsaw), 7 (1972), rpt. in Wyka, *Rzecz wyobraźni*, 2nd enlarged ed. (Warsaw, 1977), he overlooks the role of irony in "Elegy of Fortinbras" almost completely and considers the title character a proponent of the author's supposed thesis of "the superiority of the order of history and culture over any disorganization, over the order of death." Incidentally, the history of misunderstandings surrounding the "Elegy of Fortinbras" could well be the subject of a further essay, one that

would certainly tell a great deal about political illusions of Polish intellectuals after 1956.

27. A very specific case of this kind of complication can be found in poems such as "Tamarisk," "Attempt at a Description," or "Pebble," which, while they seemingly represent the form of the direct monologue, appear within the play *Reconstruction of the Poet* as monologues of Homer and thus function, in this particular context, as dramatic monologues.

28. Even before the volume *Pan Cogito* came out, certain critics had noted, on the basis of Herbert's publications in periodicals, a distinct change in his work. See, for instance, Tadeusz Polanowski, "Herberta dawne i nowe propozycje," *Tygodnik Powszechny* (Cracow), 42 (1973).

29. The inner cohesion of the sequence was emphasized, perhaps with a certain degree of exaggeration, by those critics who tended to read *Pan Cogito* as a consistent "morality play in the form of a poem" (*poemat-moralitet*) or "treatise" (*traktat*). See, for instance, Marek Jodłowski, "Antypoemat Herberta," *Odra* (Wroclaw), 7/8 (1974); Antoni Libera, "Traktat Zbigniewa Herberta," *Literatura* (Warsaw), 19 (1974). In particular, Libera examined very meticulously the inner construction of the volume, stressing the sense of purpose in its composition and the correspondences between particular poems.

30. On this subject, see particularly Ryszard Przybylski, "Oczy Pana Cogito," *Więź* (Warsaw), 11 (1974), rpt. within "Między cierpieniem a formą," in Przybylski, *To jest klasycyzm* (Warsaw, 1978).

31. On Valéry and Michaux see the interesting observations of Przybylski, "Między cierpieniem," 154–155. Bogdana and John Carpenter, "The Recent Poetry of Zbigniew Herbert," *World Literature Today,* 51 (1977), 212, strongly emphasize the difference between Mr. Cogito and Valéry's, Pound's, or Eliot's characters who represent a stable value or point of view.

32. Kwiatkowski deals with this problem in the most interesting way. Cf. his "Niezrównany Pan Cogito," in Kwiatkowski, *Felietony poetyckie* (Cracow, 1982), in which he introduces the notion of dual consciousness, borrowed from Jean-Paul Sartre. Czerniawski, "Pan Herbert Cogitans," *Oficyna Poetów* (London), 3 (1974), 19, 20, broods skeptically "on Mr. Cogito as a mask," only to come to the rather whimsical conclusion that the author "should put this intruder to death," as he "only creates confusion." Cf. polemics by Leszek Żuliński, "Czy Pan Cogito jest intruzem, którego należy uśmiercić?," *Oficyna Poetów,* 1 (1975). The questions of the relationship between the author and Mr. Cogito and the latter's identity occupied virtually all the critics who reviewed the volume *Pan Cogito.* Beside the above-mentioned, see also Henryk Jerzmański, "Świat Pana Cogito," *Życie i Myśl* (Poznan), 7 (1974); Jodłowski, "Antypoemat"; Andrzej Lam, "Kim jest pan Cogito?," *Nowe Książki* (Warsaw), 19 (1974); Libera, "Traktat"; Krzysztof Mętrak, "Prawdy Zbigniewa Herberta,"

Kultura (Warsaw), 12 (1974); Jan Pieszczachowicz, "Pana Cogito drogi wolności," *Miesięcznik Literacki* (Warsaw), 8 (1974); Marek Skwarnicki, "Smutek Pana Cogito," *Tygodnik Powszechny* (Cracow), 15 (1974); Paweł Śpiewak, "Przygody człowieczka myślącego," *Twórczość* (Warsaw), 7 (1974); Bogusław Żurakowski, "Kim jest Pan Cogito?," *Opole* (Opole), 19 (1974); Carpenter and Carpenter, "The Recent Poetry."

33. Lam, "Dialogowość poezji Herberta," *Teksty* (Warsaw), 1 (1976), 103.

34. Carpenter and Carpenter, "The Recent Poetry," 213, point out that the fluctuation between first-person and third-person presentations of the character is symbolized even by his name, in which *Pan* (Mr.) suggests a detachment, whereas *Cogito* is, significantly, a verb in the first person singular.

35. Herbert's explanation, included in a letter quoted in the above-mentioned article by Bogdana and John Carpenter, 213, only appears to be at variance with that argument: "In any case it is neither a persona nor a mask, but rather . . . a method. An attempt to isolate, to 'objectify' what is shameful, individual, and subjective. In different poems I have a different attitude toward the personage (a shorter or greater distance)" (trans. by the Carpenters).

36. Sometimes the changes occur in the opposite direction. The poem published first in *Twórczość* (Warsaw), 12 (1973), as "Mr. Cogito's Shameful Dreams" reappeared ten years later in book form simply as "Shameful Dreams" (R 33, CR 28).

37. The nature of distance as such in Herbert's poetry is paradoxical. Even before *Pan Cogito,* Kwiatkowski, "Herbert niezawodny," in Kwiatkowski, *Notatki o poezji i krytyce* (Cracow, 1975), 127, had pointed out that in Herbert's poems "distance intensifies compassion . . . but it does not cease to be distance because of that." Przybylski, "Między cierpieniem," 147, has made a few perceptive observations on the role of "the antagonism between the person and the persona" in Herbert, a phenomenon that "results from the very nature of suffering." Śpiewak, "Przygody," 118, put it more precisely: "Closeness with others is achieved [in Herbert's poetry] through distance, a distance of defense and respect . . . The irony that intensifies this feeling of distance is neither a source for accusation nor for self-humiliation here; rather, it provides the basis for a distance [that is] a sense of measure and proportion of things."

38. Mętrak, "Prawdy."

39. Bieńkowski, "Ergo," *Kultura* (Warsaw), 16 (1974), once again makes the task of interpretation easier for himself by completely ignoring those poems in which Herbert's character faces alternatives imposed on him by contemporary reality. Hence the critic's hasty generalizations: "Now Mr. Cogito preaches only the unshakeable, but also inapplicable,

truths of the catechism. He has never plunged into the depths of reality, never risked a confrontation with life," and so on.

40. Here I basically agree with the diagnosis of Błoński, "Tradycja, ironia"—which is all the more perceptive considering that it was made long before the creation of the Mr. Cogito sequence: "In Herbert's poetry *irony is a means to neutralize the incompatibility* between norms and reality, ideals and experience, tradition and the present"; to this end, irony does not turn "against values" or "against reality," but "against the point of mediation, against man, in whom the law and the fact meet; against, then, the poet himself, or, more precisely, his lyrical hero." (Błoński's italics.) I would object only to Błoński's use of the word "neutralize"; irony in Herbert, rather than neutralizing contradictions, makes them stand out even more clearly.

4. Imponderabilia

1. On the specific role of litotes as a "natural form of irony" see particularly Vladimir Jankélévitch, *L'Ironie* (Paris, 1936), 90–95.

2. Jan Prokop, "Rozmowy z Cezarem," *Więź* (Warsaw), 3 (1962).

3. Andrzej Kaliszewski, *Gry Pana Cogito* (Cracow, 1982), 107.

4. These functions of irony in Herbert have been sporadically pointed out by the critics. Jerzy Kwiatkowski, in his early essay "Klerk mężny," *Życie Literackie* (Cracow), 40 (1957), discusses the "magical defense against Stalinism" that occurs in Herbert's poetry; later, in "Imiona prostoty," in Kwiatkowski, *Klucze do wyobraźni* (Warsaw, 1964), he examines the role of litotes more closely as a "therapeutic diminution." Of foreign critics, in addition to Alfred Alvarez, Ian Hamilton, in particular, has considered Herbert's irony as "an essential strategy," thanks to which "poetry is a means of personal resistance and survival." Hamilton, "Poet from Poland," *Observer*, 2 (1968).

5. See the remarks on this poem in Bogdana and John Carpenter, "Zbigniew Herbert: The Poet as Conscience," *Slavic and East European Journal*, 1 (1980), 46–47. The authors quote their conversation with the poet, in which he admitted that Damastes bears a certain resemblance to Vladimir I. Lenin.

6. "I am interested in civilizations that died, that is, in the nations that did not succeed in history. After all, we [the Poles] have never really succeeded either." "Za nami przepaść historii," interv. Zbigniew Taranienko, *Argumenty* (Warsaw), 48 (1971). Evidence of these interests can, of course, be found in Herbert's essays as well. Of the reviewers of *Barbarian in the Garden*, Kwiatkowski, in particular, emphasized this aspect of the book most perceptively by seeing its leitmotif in the stories of "people whose

tribulations and defeats left no trace and had no career in history, as they were always inflicted by superbly efficient police systems." Kwiatkowski, "Symbol trwałości," *Życie Literackie* (Cracow), 9 (1963).

7. This way of seeing the problem is only superficially at odds with the classic approach of Søren Kierkegaard, *The Concept of Irony: With Constant Reference to Socrates,* trans. L .M. Capel (London, 1966), who stressed precisely the Socratic tradition of Romantic irony.

8. On Romantic irony see particularly Ingrid Strohschneider-Kohrs, *Die romantische Ironie in Theorie und Gestaltung* (Tübingen, 1960); Helmut Prang, *Die romantische Ironie* (Darmstadt, 1972); David Simpson, *Irony and Authority in Romantic Poetry* (London, 1979); Anne K. Mellor, *English Romantic Irony* (Cambridge, Mass., 1980).

9. Cf. especially Herbert's play *The Philosophers' Den.*

10. Jolanta Dudek appears to be wrong when she writes (before the emergence of the Mr. Cogito sequence, to be sure): "It seems that Herbert's Socrates is the most complete self-creation of the poet himself." Dudek, "Zatopiony w ciemnych promieniach ziemi . . . O poezji Zbigniewa Herberta," *Ruch Literacki* (Cracow), 5 (1971), 308. More perceptive analyses of the inner contradictions of Herbert's Socrates can be found in Karl Dedecius, "In der Höhle der Philosophen: Über Zbigniew Herbert," *Deutsche Studien* (Lüneburg), 47 (1974); Marta Piwińska, "Zbigniew Herbert i jego dramaty," *Dialog* (Warsaw), 8 (1963); Małgorzata Szpakowska, "Kuszenie Sokratesa," *Twórczość* (Warsaw), 1 (1971).

11. Konrad W. Tatarowski, "Dlaczego 'klasycy'? Próba interpretacji poezji Zbigniewa Herberta," *Zeszyty Naukowe Uniwersytetu Łódzkiego, Nauki Humanistyczno-Społeczne* (Lodz), 1, 2 (1975), 25, clearly exaggerates when he sees "Romantic irony" in poems such as "Fragment."

12. The latter fact was probably overlooked by Iwona Smolka, "W zawodnym kręgu poznania," *Twórczość* (Warsaw), 10 (1970), 105, who interprets the poems from *Napis* as an expression of Herbert's utter skepticism and even relativism: "The author's irony causes every human attitude in history to become a mask, another disguise." Zbigniew Bieńkowski's opinion, another one of his hasty generalizations, seems to be remarkably inaccurate: "Herbert . . . is open to all the arguments that beset man today . . . He knows the arguments of the tortured and the torturers. He is open to all these arguments, only to be opposed to all of them." Bieńkowski, "W środku życia," *Kultura* (Warsaw), 9 (1972). In fact, Bieńkowski contradicts himself when he says a few paragraphs later that "Herbert's irony has nothing in common with ideological indifferentism."

13. Kaliszewski, *Gry,* 27, considers "Prologue" a polemic with the poetry of Czeslaw Milosz; this supposedly appears in Herbert's stylistic references to the latter's poetics. It would be hard, however, to see the poem's primary semantic intent in that.

14. See the interpretation of this fragment in Marek Skwarnicki, "Odczytywanie 'Napisu'," *Tygodnik Powszechny* (Cracow), 12 (1970).

15. Cf. the total confusion on this matter as evidenced by one critic's statement: "Nature, the order of nature, seems to Herbert the wisest and most profound way of arranging and composing the world." Overlooking the fact that it is precisely man who is excluded from this order in Herbert's poetry, the critic blunders, by the way of a hasty analogy, into another misunderstanding: "Herbert . . . thinks that we have no right to step out of the common river-bed of history, indeed, that we are compelled to subordinate ourselves to its course, shared by all . . . History appears [to Herbert] to be a series of specific necessities . . ." Mieczysław Dąbrowski, "Program heroicznej harmonii," *Tygodnik Kulturalny* (Warsaw), 50 (1972).

16. Marcus Aurelius Antoninus, *The Meditations,* trans. John Jackson (Oxford, 1906), 68.

17. The more clear-cut choices with which Herbert confronts some of his characters, especially in his dramatic monologues, are something else again. In such cases we are dealing with a dramatic condensation rather than with an imitation of objective reality. The role of such "threshold-situations" is mentioned by George Gömöri, "Herbert and Yevtushenko: On Whose Side is History?," *Mosaic* (Winnipeg), 3 (1969), 57.

18. In his interview "Za nami przepaść historii," Herbert speaks explicitly of "the missing tables of values in the contemporary world" and of the "spiritual diminution of man."

19. Cf. his statement in another interview: "Culture's enemy number one is not censorship, but nihilism . . . This is not so much a philosophy as a state of spiritual decomposition and captivity, an absolute acceptance of everything that might happen. It is also acquiescence to the infliction of suffering on others—since everything is nothingness anyway, everything is a human corpse which will rot in the end." "Płynie się zawsze do źródeł pod prąd, z prądem płyną śmiecie (Rozmowa ze Zbigniewem Herbertem)," interv. Adam Michnik, *Krytyka* (Warsaw-London), 8 (1981), 59.

20. Diogenes Laertius, *Lives of Eminent Philosophers,* trans. R. D. Hicks, vol. 2 (London-New York, 1925), 197.

21. Cf. Ryszard Przybylski, "Między cierpieniem a formą," in Przybylski, *To jest klasycyzm* (Warsaw, 1978), 174–175.

22. I quote the translation by Czeslaw Milosz, *New York Review of Books,* 1983, no. 13.

23. Marcus Aurelius, *The Meditations,* 120.

24. Andrzej Kowalczyk, "Złote runo nicości," *Tygodnik Powszechny* (Cracow), 11 (1983). This interpretation, though otherwise interesting and persuasive owing to the author's erudition, seems both to underestimate the role of irony and tragic conflict in Herbert and to overestimate

his links with the Stoic tradition. Herbert has commented upon this tradition in other poems in a far from unequivocal fashion. Cf., for instance, characteristic formulations like "your greatness too immense" as regards Marcus Aurelius (SS 30, M 22), his depiction of Seneca as "a nice old man" who turns out to be "the deceased" ("Maturity," H 44, M 48), or the ironic treatment of "the principle of *amor fati*" in the prose poem "Mr. Cogito and the Pearl" (P 12). Words such as "equilibrium" and "harmony" linger on, incidentally, in most of the more superficial articles that touch upon the problem of Herbert's ethics. Cf. the characteristic titles of Dąbrowski, "Program heroicznej harmonii," or Zbigniew Dolecki, "Świat, historia i harmonia moralna," *Kierunki* (Warsaw), 24 (1972).

25. Henryk Elzenberg, "Brutus czyli przekleństwo cnoty," in Elzenberg, *Próby kontaktu* (Cracow, 1966).

26. Cf. Herbert's statement in an interview: "I am against the pragmatic principle [which says] that one must perform only purposeful tasks and strive for attainable goals, and that, on the other hand, unattainable goals are out of the question, that is to say, senseless. It seems to me that one undertakes a struggle not for victory's sake, because that would be too easy, and not only for the sake of struggle alone, but to defend the values that are worth living for and worth dying for." "Płynie się," 49.

27. Throwing this kind of ethics into the expansive bag of existential philosophy—which Jan Pieszczachowicz and Artur Sandauer tried to do—does not seem to explain very much. Cf. Pieszczachowicz, "Stąd do nicości (O poezji Zbigniewa Herberta)," *Współczesność* (Warsaw), 14 (1970); Sandauer, "Głos, dzielony na czworo," *Kultura* (Warsaw), 7–9 (1976), rpt. in Sandauer, *Zebrane pisma krytyczne,* vol. 1 (Warsaw, 1981).

28. Such is, for example, Krzysztof Dybciak's observation, "W poszukiwaniu istoty i utraconych wartości," in Dybciak, *Gry i katastrofy* (Warsaw, 1980), 155. However, Dybciak rather incorrectly adds "Buddhist elements" to that tradition; if Buddhist thought is mentioned in Herbert's poetry at all, it appears, as a rule, as the object of ironical polemics (cf. especially "Pan Cogito a myśl czysta," P 20–21).

29. Cf. Herbert's confession in one of his interviews: "I invented this kind of practical moral directive for my private use: If you have two paths to choose, choose always the path that is more difficult for you. And besides, I believe that there are beautiful and ugly things, good and bad things, noble and base things. And woe betide those structures in which these borderlines become blurred in the name of anything at all." "Jeśli masz dwie drogi . . . Rozmowa ze Zbigniewem Herbertem," interv. Krystyna Nastulanka, *Polityka* (Warsaw), 9 (1972), rpt. in Nastulanka, *Sami o sobie: Rozmowy z pisarzami i uczonymi* (Warsaw, 1975), 286.

30. Leszek Kołakowski, "Etyka bez kodeksu," *Twórczość* (Warsaw), 7 (1962), rpt. in Kołakowski, *Kultura i fetysze* (Warsaw, 1967).

31. Jan Józef Szczepański, "W służbie Wielkiego Armatora," in Szczepański, *Przed nieznanym trybunałem* (Warsaw, 1975), 13.

32. Elzenberg, *Kłopot z istnieniem: Aforyzmy w porządku czasu* (Cracow, 1963), 143.

33. Cf. Elzenberg's note of 1910: "*The tragic* as an ethics, the essence of life, the overcoming of pessimism. It *arises* from pessimism and at the same time removes it." Ibid., 35 (Elzenberg's italics).

34. Dybciak, "W poszukiwaniu," 155, makes a pertinent remark on Herbert's resistance to "the ethics of efficiency" (*przeciwko etyce sprawności*). The best illustration of this attitude can be found in the poet's essay "Węzeł gordyjski" [The Gordian Knot], *Więź* (Warsaw), 6 (1981), 45, in which the legendary gesture of Alexander the Great is interpreted as a legitimization of brute force.

35. Kwiatkowski, "Po platońsku," in Kwiatkowski, *Felietony poetyckie* (Cracow, 1982), 180. Cf. also the more detailed exposition of this subject in Dybciak, "W poszukiwaniu." Dybciak deserves credit for, among other things, having paid a great deal of attention to the numerous essays and short articles that Herbert published between 1955 and 1956 in *Twórczość* monthly; these critical exercises had a significant impact on the shaping of the poet's aesthetic options.

36. Its role has been stressed particularly by Jan Błoński, "Tradycja, ironia i głębsze znaczenie," *Poezja* (Warsaw), 3 (1970), 26.

37. Cf. Jan Prokop's remarks on the "antirhetoricality" of Herbert's poems, which is reflected in his conversational style. Prokop, "Epitafium dla duszyczki," in Prokop, *Lekcja rzeczy* (Cracow, 1972), 186n.

38. The parallel between Arcadia and Utopia is interestingly illuminated in Herbert's brief essay of 1956 on the work of A. A. Milne: "The idyll's necessary condition is a construction of conventional reality done in such a way that beyond it no other reality can be sensed. Happy islands must be perfectly isolated, impermeable, tightly closed to outside dramas. Hence the feeling of security that the idyll's reader enjoys.

"This essential feature—isolation—is shared by both the idyll and the utopia. But over utopian islands a cold, rational sun shines and life there is hampered by meticulous regulations, as in Campanella, where emotional matters are superintended by a Minister of Love. Over idyllic islands a more humane weather reigns. There, the issue at stake is not, as in utopias, a system or organization, but the removal of the factors that poison the taste of man's life, his simple occupations, simple food and simple joy." Herbert, "A. A. Milne (1882–1956)," *Twórczość* (Warsaw), 4 (1956), 203–204. The existence of this essay was first noted by Dybciak, "W poszukiwaniu," 157–158.

39. The way this kind of skepticism hurts the feelings of the Marxist critic is typical. Bogusław Sławomir Kunda, for instance, thundered: "Mr.

Cogito's inventory of instructions does not include recommendations to unveil and eradicate the sources of evil." Kunda, "Pan Cogito czyli pułapki moralistyki," *Życie Literackie* (Cracow), 33 (1974).

40. "Płynie się," 57.

41. See Thomas More, *Utopia,* trans. Paul Turner (Harmondsworth: Penguin Books, 1980), 84.

42. Wisława Szymborska, "Utopia," in Szymborska, *Wielka liczba* (Warsaw, 1976). English translation in Szymborska, *Sounds, Feelings, Thoughts,* trans. Magnus J. Krynski and Robert Maguire (Princeton, 1981).

Index